Cucina Povera

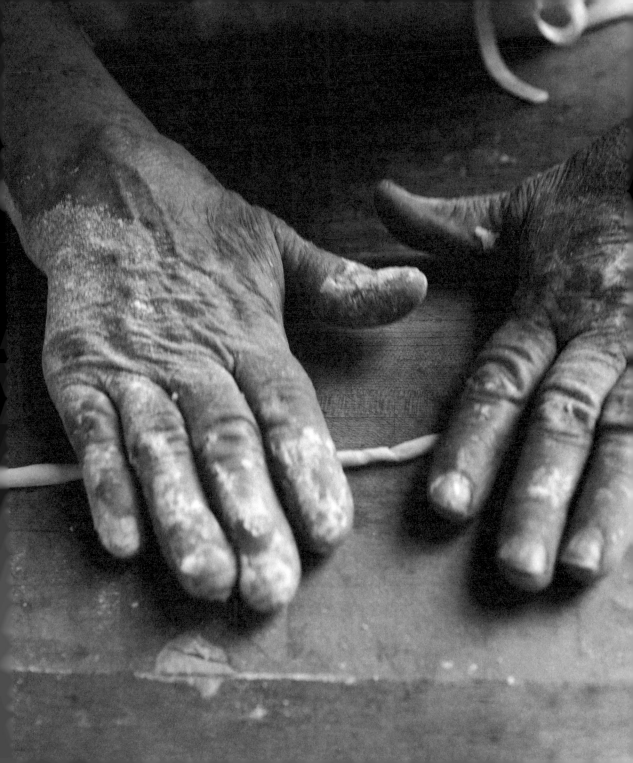

Cucina Povera

TUSCAN PEASANT COOKING

PAMELA SHELDON JOHNS

Photographs by
ANDREA WYNER

**Andrews McMeel
Publishing, LLC**
Kansas City • Sydney • London

Dedicated to Edna and Alvin Sheldon
At the core of this book is a statement that may be the most important for me:
When life starts simple, influences from the outside world don't change it much.
My parents taught me this, and I thank them.

Andrews McMeel Publishing, LLC
an Andrews McMeel Universal company
1130 Walnut Street, Kansas City, Missouri 64106
www.andrewsmcmeel.com

11 12 13 14 15 TEN 10 9 8 7 6 5 4 3 2 1

ISBN: 978-1-4494-0238-9

Library of Congress Control Number: 2010937753

Packaged and designed by Jennifer Barry Design, Fairfax, California
Photography: Andrea Wyner
Food styling: Pamela Sheldon Johns
Layout production: Kristen Hall
Cartography: Ben Pease, Pease Press, San Francisco, California
Copyediting: Carolyn Miller

www.foodartisans.com

Corpo pieno, anima consolata.

If your stomach is full, your spirit will be calm.

Table of Contents

Preface

My mother grew up on a farm in the Midwest during the Great Depression. I think she was haunted all of her life about never quite having enough. She wasn't necessarily frugal, but she never wasted a thing. All the extra fruits and vegetables from our garden were put up in cans. Every empty jar was reused. Leftovers found a place of honor on the next day's table.

I inherited this tendency, it seems. I hate throwing away anything that can be used again, whether it is food, the odd screw or nail, or products that can be recycled. I humbly submit that I am an expert at creating something from nothing, whether it is a craft project or a dinner made with bits of leftovers and an egg.

This attitude was reinforced when I moved to Tuscany; I felt as if I were reborn into the mentality of no waste. Here, so many people still remember the dire poverty of the times before, during, and just after World War II. My friends and neighbors were not impressed with my jars of jam in summer; rather, they raised their eyebrows at the sight of any fruit left on the ground. Any conversation about the traditional dishes here eventually turns into stories and remembrances of how precious each bread crumb was in the past.

Living in Tuscany has also helped me understand how simple dishes have earned a permanent place in today's cuisine by their reliance on fresh and seasonal local ingredients, foods foraged from the land, and inexpensive cuts of meat. These are the tenets for good food in hard times. I hope they will serve you as well.

Introduction
Food Memories of the Cobbler of Montepulciano

"You want to know about cucina povera? *Ahhhhh, I was bred on that. My mother would go out in the countryside and pick the* cicoria *and* puntarelle, *the same ones that are growing wild out in your field (similar to dandelion greens) . . . just the tender tips, and then she would chop them and make a frittata. Ohhh. That was in the spring, when we had more eggs than she could sell. That was the time when the first salame was ready to eat, still pink and heady with the aroma of fennel seed and sweet meat. Pasqua (Easter) was the best. We really ate until we were full. On those days, we could imagine what it meant to eat like kings." —Virio Neri*

Since 2001, Virio Neri, the *calzolaio* (cobbler) of Montepulciano, has been part of our family in a case of mutual adoption. He not only fills the role of grandfather for my daughter, but he has also brought Italian culture to life for us in an intimate way, sharing personal stories and remembrances of his life in our small hill town. The smell of a *ciambellone* (a simple cake, page 156) fresh from the oven can send him into a reverie about his mother's *stufa economica*, the wood stove that she rose early every day to light with twigs and hay and hard wood that Virio cut exactly to size for her.

"Oh! The fava beans, fresh with a bit of *marzolino* [the first sheep's milk cheese of the season], the chestnuts, and the chickpeas! We survived on these. Do you know how many figs I ate? Sometimes my mother would put an almond or a walnut in a dried fig and warm it in the wood oven. Heaven.

"The best," he continued, "the very best, was the *pan' santo* [page 48]. We would dip some dry bread in broth, then put boiled cavolo nero [dinosaur or lacinato kale] on top, and a blessing of oil. We'd have that for dinner, and sometimes also for lunch. My mother would say, '*Corpo pieno, anima consolata,*' which means 'If your stomach is full, your spirit will be calm.'"

Virio, now in his late seventies, practically swoons when he talks about this food. It makes you wonder about his exceptionally positive memories, because he grew up in a time of poverty and intense hunger. Perhaps desire made the food taste better. Perhaps those simple, pure flavors are harder to find now.

Cucina Buona in Tempi Brutti
Good Food for Hard Times

Italy, a country now recognized for its excellent food, has a disturbing history of malnutrition and hunger, mainly sustained by the now-abolished class and sharecropping system known as *mezzadria*. While the land-owners consumed a greater variety of food and nourishing proteins, the working class subsisted on what they could glean from their meager rations and gather from the land.

From these hard times came recipes that have endured and have even become exalted. More than the recipes, *la cucina povera*, "the cooking of the poor," or "peasant cooking," is based on the philosophy of not wasting anything edible and using a variety of simple techniques to make every bite as tasty as possible. It is a cuisine of ingenious creativity in using next to nothing while maintaining a reverence for everything. This lifestyle is not limited to Italy, of course: It has touched every culture that has ever been affected by war, famine, poverty, or natural disaster.

Our adopted *nonno* (grandfather), Virio, lived through hard times in the late 1930s and the 1940s, when, like his fellow Tuscan countrymen, he survived by foraging, hunting, and living off the land. The period before, during, and after World War II was a time of great poverty in Italy. Stomachs were only ever full then on the rare special occasion of a wedding or a funeral. Very little meat was available, and the preservation of food was more than an art, it was a prerequisite for survival.

Virio recalls that on the way to school every day, he would stop in front of the *alimentari*, the tiny neighborhood grocery store, and grab a handful of chestnut flour from the bag that was open for customers to scoop out their desired amount. "The owner would look the other way . . . that bit of flour was my breakfast, so sweet and satisfying."

In Tuscany, many people survived on chestnut flour in those times. The chestnuts from wild trees are a food that can be gathered and preserved by drying. Once dried, the shelled chestnut is ground. The flour is sweet, and while it doesn't have enough gluten to make bread with, it was used for polenta on a daily basis. Even though poor in protein, chestnuts provide carbohydrates for energy, along with some vitamin C. By contrast, field corn, imported from North America, created nutritional devastation in northern Italy in the 1800s in the form of a disease called pellagra, which is caused by a deficit of niacin in a corn-intensive diet. Unlike the Mayans and ancient American cultures, the Italians had not learned to treat corn with lime, a process that alleviates the niacin deficiency.

At the beginning of the twentieth century, most people lived in the countryside in *case coloniche*, farmhouses that sheltered extended families consisting of as many as ten to fifteen people. In these homes, the focal point was the kitchen, the room with the fireplace, which was not only a source of heat for cooking but also for warmth. At the end of a hard day of work, the family gathered on benches around the fire for conversation and story telling.

Il Focolare
THE HEARTH, CENTER OF THE PEASANT KITCHEN

In many homes, the cooking was done in the fireplace in large pots suspended by blackened chains that could raise or lower the pots to control the cooking temperature. Women stirred wheat, chestnut, or corn polenta in a copper pot over the wood fire, being careful not to lose one bit of precious food sticking to the pot. Virio remembers that the occasional ashes in the pot added a particular flavor, along with the fragrance of wood smoke.

"My mother had a *madia*, a large wooden chest where flour was kept, and where dough was kneaded and left to rise. On Thursdays, she took the loaves to the communal oven to be baked, and that lasted us the whole week."

Tuscan bread is not made with salt because up until a few years ago, salt was heavily taxed and was used only for the things that were absolutely necessary such as curing meat and making cheese; none was spared for bread. In any event, bread was baked only once a week, and bread made without salt dries out within a day, as salt is what holds the moisture in the bread. From these simple facts come the many classic Italian recipes that use dry or day-old bread, such as *ribollita* (page 71), *panzanella* (page 81), and *pappa al pomodoro* (page 67). Virio remembers: "We loved the bread fresh from the community oven. My mother would take the dough there in the morning and put her mark on it. At noon, she would go back to pick it up. She would only let us have one piece because the bread had to last all week, and the next day it was already dry. We sometimes soaked it in water, milk, or even wine."

La Prima Colazione
Breakfast, a Ladle of Milk, and a Prayer

Breakfast was often a piece of dry or day-old bread softened in hot milk (or water, if there was no cow) and sometimes a few grains of sugar. In the winter, when there was more time to stir and to spoil the children a bit, there was sometimes sweet polenta with milk. In the summer and fall, however, on the days when there was wheat to harvest or thresh and no time to even start the fire, a simple *panino* of *salume* would give energy. At the height of summer, when there was an abundance of garden produce that couldn't be preserved, such as potatoes, cabbage, or other greens, the leftover soup from the night before would be reheated for breakfast.

Le Quattro Stagioni
The Four Seasons, Cooking and Eating in Season

Today, we know that the best produce is local and seasonal. In Virio's youth, it was the only produce available. Each month had its specialty, and just as now, people looked forward to strawberries in the spring, peaches in the summer, and porcini in the fall.

For the *contadino* (farmer), the agricultural year followed a fixed schedule, and seasonal dishes were the result. In January, after months of fattening, the pig was slaughtered. Days of labor were needed to turn the animal into salume, sausages, and cooked *soppressata*. The prime cuts went to the property owner. The hind legs became prosciutto, the front legs became *spalla*. Other large whole pieces, such as the loin (*lombo*), belly (*pancetta*), and neck (*coppa*) also needed to be salted and massaged and hung to dry. Small pieces of meat and fat were chopped to be fresh sausage or dried to be salame. In any case, there was always some fresh meat to roast or grill, and this was a real treat in the winter.

This was also the time that the drying grapes were pressed to make vin santo. In the cold winter months, when there wasn't work in the fields, meals were made from the garden produce that had been dried, smoked, or preserved in vinegar, salt, or oil. Soup with dried beans and a piece of pancetta or the usual polenta was a staple, warming and filling.

As early as March, the men went out to plow the land to prepare it for the new crops. With the coming of spring, fava beans, peas, and artichokes graced the table. Eggs were abundant, and soon asparagus and strawberries arrived. Work intensified with the planting. Although the work was hard, it was welcome after the months inside. The colors of the countryside turned from the lilac of wisteria and wild iris to the fiery red of poppies. The women planted summer seeds and scared away the birds as the seedlings came up.

Summer was a time of bounty, but also of work, including for the women who did the cooking. Often, lunch consisted of a hearty *panino* (sandwich), sometimes with a piece of cheese and some garden vegetables marinated in vinegar. During snail season in June and July, the creatures were captured and kept in a cage supplied with fresh greens every day for forty days to purge and clean them before they were cooked.

In the fall, weather permitting, porcini mushrooms might be foraged on Sundays to grace the top of the polenta. At harvest time, a goose was often roasted and consumed over several meals: The intestines, liver, and stomach were served as toppings for bruschetta (toasted bread), the feet for pasta sauce, and the bones for soup to give the men strength and protein for the *trebbiatura* (wheat harvest and threshing).

Once the grapes were harvested in the fall, field work slowed down and it was time for hunting birds and rabbits and larger game such as wild boar and deer. The chestnuts ripened and fell from the trees; there was jam to be made from figs; and there were walnuts to gather. After some rain followed by a couple of days of sun, mushrooms were begging to be picked for grilling, sautéing, or preserving in oil.

Starting in November, the olives were harvested and ground into precious oil. The *raccolta* (olive harvest) was a time of celebration, not only of the new oil, but of the end of the hard work for the year.

OLIVE OIL

In the twenty years that I have been studying olive oil production, and even in the ten that I have been making my own olive oil, I have seen the season and the technique of making olive oil change drastically.

In the past, farmers waited until the last possible minute to harvest, allowing the olives to mature as much as possible, and harvesting them just before temperatures turned to freezing, sometimes as late as December or early January. The oil may have been fruitier, but it wasn't as fresh tasting as it is now.

The trend these days is to pick earlier, striving for a pizzico, the burn in the back of the throat that is an acquired taste and a prized characteristic of Tuscan oil.

The pizzico is present in a variety of olive called coreggiolo, but can also be achieved from an immature olive of any variety, hence the earlier picking.

Extraction methods have changed as well. The stone-ground olive paste is no longer stacked on straw mats and pressed; instead more hygienic methods are used to macerate and extract the oil under conditions that inhibit oxidation. This processing lowers the acidity and produces a fresher oil that tastes better and lasts longer.

As it is today, the raccolta (olive harvest) in the past was a time of celebration because the hardest work was done for the year. A lighted fire, toasted bread, new oil drizzled on top—it doesn't get much better than that.

Le Memorie
MEMORIES

Following are stories from some of my other Tuscan friends about how they managed in hard times. We begin with the rolling hills where I live, then a city visit, then up into the Apennine and Apuane Mountains, then down to the sea, south to the Maremma, and finally back home to Montepulciano. Each area had a different experience in hard times, but throughout Italy the story was the same: making do with inexpensive local foods.

Artimino
COOKING AND ECONOMIA RURALE

Our first stop is in Artimino, just northeast of Florence, to visit chef Carlo Cioni, my original icon of *cucina povera*. I met Carlo at his restaurant Da Delfina in 1992 and learned for the first time about the peasant cooking of the past. At that time, Carlo's mother, Delfina, was still alive, shelling peas and ironing tablecloths for the restaurant. She died last year, at the age of 101.

Delfina was not only the namesake of the restaurant, she was the original chef, starting at the nearby Medici hunting lodge, then eventually opening her own establishment. She was the inspiration for the kind of cooking that Carlo has masterfully carried on, a cuisine based on the careful use of ingredients, an attention to flavor, and a respect for tradition. Something that Carlo told me when I first met him still holds true: "Today's choice of simple foods is not out of necessity as it was in the past. Now, in addition to considering economy, we are seeking quality and purity of flavor."

Carlo calls his cooking *economia rurale*, "rural economy," an approach that emphasizes local, natural, and seasonal foods. He is just as happy foraging in the fields around his restaurant as he is cooking what he finds. A bright smile flashes in his tanned face as he grabs a handful of wild borage or fennel. "We can eat the borage flowers in a salad and dry the fennel flowers to sprinkle on roasted meats. The land has a lot to give; you just have to look." In his kitchen garden, he grows the essential *aromi* (flavors) of the Tuscan kitchen: carrots, celery, and onions. Herbs, cultivated and wild, abound, as does seasonal produce like cavolo nero, which he will use in the fall for *ribollita* (page 71). Carlo's *ribollita* is a classic example of the economy of this cuisine. *Ribollita* literally means "reboiled," and is a traditional Tuscan dish that exemplifies the frugality and resourcefulness of Tuscan cooks in using leftover ingredients.

Il Casentino
THE SIMPLE LIFE

The Casentino is an area in the Apennines above Arezzo. Long the domain of woodcutters, charcoal-makers, and shepherds, the land provides highly acclaimed cultivated foods, cured meat products, and foraged and hunted delicacies. The potatoes, tomatoes, and corn are exceptional. Mushrooms, boar, and hare are traditional seasonal fare; trout, eel, and frog are appreciated as well. The local pork breed called Casentinese, which is raised on the wild forage of oaks and chestnut trees, is transformed into treasures such as *rigatino* (pancetta), *migliaccio* (blood sausage), and prosciutto.

The *prosciutti* are salted and air-dried for several months; these hams are unique for their spice blend, which contains the usual salt, garlic, and pepper, but also *peperoncino* (red pepper), nutmeg, and ground juniper berries. After about fifty days of cleaning and salting, the *prosciutti* are then hung in a room with a fireplace to lightly smoke for a few months.

The old ways are still evident in these mountains. Many ancient water mills have survived the ages, and several are still working. At the heart of it all is a religious sanctuary that also has not changed much in five hundred years.

When your life is based on simple premises, influences from the outside world don't alter it greatly. Tucked in the mountains of the Casentino above Arezzo, at the border of Tuscany and Romagna, is the source of the Arno, one of Tuscany's principal rivers. Nearby, an order of monks has found sanctuary since the year 1012. In the solitude of this faraway place, they have raised food to a higher order for the glory of God, by honoring their own well-being and that of the local people in frugal ways that are genuine and natural, always respecting tradition. The Camaldoli monks find spirituality in the environment and in nature, using healing combinations of plants and herbs in recipes dating back to 1510. In that year, the monastery's botanical garden began providing material for the pharmacy, which is still equipped with its original distillery, mortars, stoves, and antique documents.

The Casentino valley is the site of an immense forest of maple, ash, elm, fir, beech, and chestnut trees. Considered a sacred place in Etruscan times, the forest has been tended by the Camaldoli monks for centuries. For the monks, the forest was and is a natural temple. Their codex, a sixteen-thousand-page document spanning seven hundred years, is on file in the State Archives in Florence and used by modern agronomists as a natural forestry guide. The Casentino, now a national park, is where Dante wandered while writing *The Divine Comedy* during the first years of his exile. It was also a retreat for St. Francis, who, in 1224,

received the stigmata at nearby La Verna. Today, the forest is a lush habitat for deer, wild boar, wolves, and many different species of birds, including the golden eagle.

Between the Camaldoli and the Franciscans, this has long been a religious destination, with pilgrims passing through and very likely bringing with them plants to add to the monastery garden. Today, as in the past, the monks produce distilled liqueurs and cordials that have been infused without heating and can be sipped or added to sparkling water after a meal to aid digestion and improve health. All infusions are made with organic plants and herbs grown and gathered from the monastery garden. Over the centuries, the monks have learned that certain plants have healing properties, such as rosemary for vision, eucalyptus for coughs, verbena for depression, echinacea for allergies, chamomile for relaxation, and dandelion root for digestion. Bee propolis and honeys are produced for their antibiotic and antibacterial properties, and are recommended for respiratory problems, sore throats, and colds.

HERBAL REMEDIES

For more than five hundred years, the Camaldoli monks of the Casentino have been cultivating organic herbs and plants for remedies designed to restore equilibrium to the body. Here are some of the combinations used to make teas or liqueurs that aid insomnia, indigestion, and other physical maladies, accompanied by their words of wisdom regarding the ailments.

THE ARTICHOKE BLEND (liver)

"Not everything you eat is always tolerated by the liver." Artichoke, combretum (bush-willow), elder, rapontico (rhubarb), karkadè (hibiscus flower), smaller centaurea (cornflower), sweet-smelling asperula (woodruff), elicriso (curry plant), rosemary, chicory, licorice, and sweet orange.

Antica Farmacia
dei Monaci Camaldolesi
Camaldoli - Arezzo

OAK BLEND (overweight)

"It pleases no one to travel the road with a very heavy backpack, with kilos in excess." Oak, ash, mountain rhamnus (buckthorn), sage, quinine, birch, licorice, equiseto (horse-tail), fennel, mint, achillea millefoglie (yarrow), red grapes, juniper berries, asparagus, sweet orange, and lemon.

MELISSA BLEND (sleep)

"Even if you sleep well without this herb tea, you will sleep better with it." Melissa, linden, hawthorn, chamomile, sweet-smelling verbena, sweet-smelling asperula (woodruff), hops, orange, and poppies.

EUCALYPTUS BLEND (sleep/cough)

"For the desperate sleep of one who coughs." Eucalyptus, chamomile, licorice, fennel, mint, malva (mallow), colts-foot, pine, lichen, verbasco (mullein), centaurea (cornflower), primrose, poppy, and broom.

FENNEL BLEND (digestion)

"After a meal that was too plentiful, or in case of heaviness, a good digestive is noteworthy." Fennel, mint, linden, licorice, sweet orange, bellflower, rosemary, melissa, hyssop, orange, karkadè (hibiscus flower), centaurea (cornflower), and lavender.

WILD GRASS BLEND (constipation)

"In nature there exists the solution to the problem of constipation: healthy nutrition, movement, and a good herb tea." Cassius obtusifolia (cassia seed), wild grass, mint, bardana (burdock), parietaria, chamomile, coriander, fennel, melissa summit, sarsaparilla, and star anise.

Colognora
Castagno Sacro, the Sacred Chestnut

High in the sparsely populated mountains above the town of Collodi, in the province of Lucca, the winding road called *la via delle cartiere* meanders through lush woods to arrive at the tiny village of Colognora. *Via delle cartiere* means "the road of the paper makers" and is lined with paper mills. In the 1700s, this area was a thriving source of paper made from straw. Now, some of the structures are in ruin, their large grinding stones left abandoned, but some are still active, with mountains of recycled paper waiting to be processed

by modern machinery.

Colognora is eighteen hundred feet above sea level and quite distant from big-city life. There is a complete sense of stepping back in time, from the demeanor of the residents to the lack of twenty-first-century trappings.

To the mountain dwellers of the past, the chestnut tree was a gift in every aspect of their existence. Nothing was wasted; it could be considered the symbol of *cucina povera*. The nut was eaten fresh or dried and ground for flour; the shells were used for fuel to dry the chestnuts. The dark, pungent honey from the chestnut flowers was eaten with the fresh local ricotta. The best wood of the tree was used for building, barrels, furniture, and hand tools. Lesser-quality wood was used for fencing and posts, thin shaved pieces became baskets, and the leftover bits of wood were turned into slow-burning charcoal used in the forging of knives and sharp tools. The tannins extracted from the wood were employed to tan leather. The fresh leaves, along with old chestnuts and acorns, were used for animal feed, and in the autumn the fallen leaves were used to line the stalls in place of hay, which was used in the paper mills.

There are several varieties of the *castagno*, as the chestnut tree is called in Italian, but the *farina dolce*, or sweet flour, in this area comes from the Carpinesi variety. These wild trees were pruned and tended as if they were part of an orchard.

I met with three elderly women who grew up in these mountains, Eni Fiorini Marcucci (born in 1921), her cousin, Meri Franceschi (born in 1932), in Colognora; and Lucia Andreotti (born in 1936) from Piteglio in the mountains above Pistoia. All three endured difficult times, especially after the war, but with the chestnut they always had food to eat. Foraging was and is a way of life, with an abundance of mushrooms and game found in the woods. At home, they cultivated beans and potatoes, and made pecorino and ricotta cheese from the milk of their hardy mountain sheep.

Their peaceful life was disrupted by the war. Signora Lucia recalls seeing white bread, chewing gum (*cingomma*), and chocolate for the first time in her life when the American soldiers arrived. At that time, local bread was made from chestnut flour only, except in the short spring season for *marzolo*, a wheat planted in small amounts in March. And though there was wheat grain (farro, in fact), just a few kilometers away in the Garfagnana, that was too far: "You would have to take a mule over there, and it just wasn't practical."

Signora Eni, who lives forty kilometers from Piteglio, remembers that the Germans brought flour for her and her mother to make bread. If they brought five kilos of flour, they expected five kilos of bread in return. "But everyone knows that five kilos of flour makes more than five kilos of bread, because you add the weight of the water to it—so we always had some bread left over for ourselves."

The daily food was *necci*, a type of crêpe made with chestnut flour. Signore Lucia and Eni may be the last two women who still make them in the traditional way on stone disks heated in a fireplace, though one man has taken it upon himself to carry the tradition on.

Sauro Petroni was born in Colognora in 1957. In his life, he has seen many changes in the way people eat and how food is handled. The traditional process of working with chestnuts has become mechanized and distant. To hear him reminisce about his childhood with his neighbor Signora Eni, you might think that much of the past was spent working with the chestnuts and dancing. "We danced a lot," Signora Eni says and smiles, "and when my husband got tired, I still danced with my friends." It was a good release from the hard work.

In the summer, the women wove bags of hemp to be used for gathering the chestnuts. Supplies were procured from the Pescia market, fifteen kilometers distant, and bartered for with chestnut products or the money earned by the men working in the paper mills. In the late summer, using a scythe, the men would prune the trees and clean the forest floor to prepare for the harvest of the nuts, which took place in October. Leaves would also be gathered and dried for later use in making *necci* in the winter.

After the backbreaking work of gathering the nuts from the ground, the chestnuts were taken to dry in the *metato*, a stone-walled room or small building with two levels, typically with a roof made of chestnut beams and with thin strips of chestnut wood dividing the two rooms. Inside smoldered a small, slow fire of chestnut husks saved from previous harvests. The fire was kept stoked for two to three months, and as the chestnuts dried on the upper floor, they would shrink inside the shell, making it easy to remove the shell. At this point, the nuts were taken to the miller, who ground them with millstones to a fine flour.

Sauro has become an expert *necci* maker under Signora Eni's tutelage. He lights a fire in his hearth with small pieces of dry wood—not chestnut wood, however, as he needs a fast, hot fire. Next to the fireplace is a wooden tower, the *reggipiastre*, that holds the *testi*, round stones about six inches in diameter and an inch thick. These stones are put over the fire to heat, held by two horizontal metal rods. While the stones are heating, Sauro blends the chestnut flour with water in a wooden bowl to a paste the consistency of thick pancake batter. Signora Eni recommends a tiny pinch of salt in a year when the chestnuts are not as sweet as usual. "Too much salt lifts the sweetness, but when the chestnut flour isn't so sweet, you need it."

When Sauro is ready to make the *necci*, he puts the first heated stone back in its tower and places a chestnut leaf on the stone. In the summer, the *necci* are made with fresh chestnut leaves; in the winter, the dried leaves are soaked in water for a few hours to soften them, then patted dry. A large spoonful of the batter is placed directly on the leaf and covered with another leaf. At once, Sauro places another hot stone on top and repeats the process until the stones are stacked in a tower with the *necci* in between. After a few minutes, the *necci* have cooked and the leaves are peeled off. Their sweet smell is redolent of the forest, and when the crêpes are wrapped around fresh ricotta cheese, the taste is sublime.

Today in the Apennines, many people still make *necci* over a fire using *testi di ferro*, long-handled metal disks oiled with a piece of pork fat, but they are also made in a nonstick pan on the stove. Instructions for making *necci* on the stovetop can be found on page 58.

Throughout these beautiful mountains, in view of the Apuan peaks that hold precious marble quarries, there are many interpretations of hearth breads and their variations. Some use chestnut flour, while others use wheat or corn. In the far northwest part of Tuscany, in an area called Lunigiana, the specialty is *testaroli*, a wheat flour crêpe cooked on a flat terra-cotta or iron pan called a *testo*; the cooked *testarolo* is cut into strips, then boiled, and served as a pasta. Besides *necci* and breads, dishes using chestnuts and chestnut flour are numerous and are still an essential part of the mountain table: *castagnaccio*, a dense pudding-like cake seasoned with rosemary and pine nuts (page 155); *mondine*, fresh roasted chestnuts;

Antico Molino di Sotto

In the past, each community in Italy had its own grain mill. In the village of Pieve Fosciana in the Garfagnana, the Molino di Sotto, or lower mill, was built in the 1700s by the municipality. At the time, there were two mills, one above (sopra), and one below (sotto). The upper mill was turned into accommodations for the millers. Since the early 1800s, four generations of the Regoli family have operated the mill, starting with Regolo Regoli, the great-grandfather of Ercolano, the current miller, who has worked in the mill since he was fifteen years old.

The current mill has four grinding stones: two *arenaria* for chestnuts and two *focaia* for corn and farro. The wheels are powered by a strong stream and fitted with wooden paddles that can be regulated to control the amount of water entering the mill, and therefore the speed of the grinding wheel.

First, the grains are dried; the chaff is then removed by use of the *ventola*, the same hand-cranked tool used one hundred years ago. The cleaned grain is then stored until ready to grind. When an order comes in for freshly ground meal, Ercolano's wife, Maria Assunta Raffaelle, spreads the grains out on a large piece of fabric under the sun to eliminate any moisture.

*balloccio *, dried chestnuts soaked in milk overnight, then boiled with bay leaves and wild fennel for two hours (locally called *tullore*); *vinata*, a kind of polenta made with watered-down wine pressings and chestnut flour; and finally polenta. Chestnut polenta (page 82) was eaten every day during hard times, as Signora Eni remembers: "Polenta at night and polenta the next morning for breakfast."

La Garfagnana
A Tradition of Corn and Farro

Working our way through the mountain passes, westward-bound toward the sea, we pass through the Garfagnana, a zone unique for the richness of its food. One of the products that thrives here is called *formenton di otto file*, a red or yellow corn with eight rows of kernels, similar to the Indian corn of the United States. Corn in the Americas is one of the most manipulated foods in the world. What we find in the little valley of the Serchio River of the Garfagnana, and in a few other areas of northern Italy, is probably very much like the original corn that arrived from Mexico in the 1500s. This type of corn produces only 12 percent of the yield of today's hybridized corn crops, which have been modified to have a higher yield. The aroma and flavor of the freshly ground *formenton* is rich with the essence of corn, unlike the finely machine-ground degerminated cornmeal found in supermarkets today.

Formenton is not a sweet corn to be eaten fresh; instead it is a field corn that is dried and stone ground to make a number of dishes, especially polenta. Corn is not indigenous to Italy, and even though chestnut flour polenta preceded corn polenta by centuries, corn polenta has become iconic in Italian cuisine. Other dishes are made as well, including *mana fregoli*, a creamy cooked cornmeal served with milk or cream for breakfast; *frittele*, or cornmeal fritters; cookies; and *vinata*, made with wine pressings.

Every step of the *formenton* production process is organic and hands on. The corn is air-dried, the cobs are degrained by hand, and the grain is stone ground slowly with a water-driven mill so that the grain doesn't heat up, which guards both flavor and nutrition.

The Garfagnana is also famous for farro, an ancient strain of wheat, *Triticum dicoccum*, which at one time was near extinction. An important food source even in Etruscan times, this grain is high in protein and has a rich, nutty flavor. A typical meal in the past might have included farro boiled in milk or water with fennel, but today the most well-known dishes are *zuppa di farro*, a soup made with white beans and sometimes potatoes (page 65), and *insalata di farro*, a salad of farro and garden vegetables (page 78). In Garfagnana, farro is also used to make bread, pasta, beer, and even *necci*.

Pozzi di Pietrasanta
Between the Mountains and the Sea

The drive down to the Ligurian Sea is stunningly beautiful. The road parallels the Via del Sale, the Salt Road, once a simple path for people coming to trade salt for chestnut flour. Many of the villages here have been nearly abandoned as people have sought less difficult lives and work in the cities. The visitor can sense an eerie presence of the not-so-long-ago war that devastated the simple quality of life in this area, which became the *linea gotica* (the Gothic Line), the front lines of the last battles of World War II.

Pietrasanta is at the foot of the Apuane Alps, in the center of coastal Versilia. When I asked if people with access to the riches of the sea fared better than others during the war, Ilvana Corsi Tognocchi, born in 1925, straightened me out right away: "We were forbidden to go to the water or out in boats for military security reasons. The best we could do was an occasional bucket of sea water to boil down for the salt."

Signora Ilvana's cousin Ivano Leonardi (born in 1934) was just ten years old during the war, but it left him with enduring memories. "The Nazis were encamped at a neighbor's farm. They took a walk every night past our door and asked for a glass of wine in trade for cigarettes. We had to sip the wine first to show that it hadn't been poisoned." Ivano's wife, Renza del Bianco (born in 1938), was just a child, but she remembers that the Germans slaughtered a cow and left the head behind: "We were hungry at home; I started dragging the head down the road, and a couple of big boys tried to take it. A German officer saw what was happening and ran them off. I made it home with the head, and my mother made soup."

Signora Ilvana's father was a butcher, but they rarely had more than a bit of meat to flavor their soup. "I remember we first ate polenta with plenty of olive oil and Pecorino cheese . . . then we ate it with just oil . . . and then just polenta, sometimes cooked in milk for the kids. Polenta. Polenta every day. We had to work all day to get our daily ration of two hundred grams of bread," she said. "We ate carob beans . . . horse food! I remember eating spaghetti and beans a lot. My mother told me to be thrifty with the oil. I had to drizzle it on sparingly in a figure eight instead of the usual amount." They were creative, using *bossole*, or empty bomb casings, for cooking pots and secretly burying demijohns of grain to hide it. Some demijohns had to be left out to avoid suspicion. "The Germans didn't like corn. We would fill the demijohns with grain, then put some corn on top to make it appear as if it were full of corn."

Signora Ilvana's good friend Diana Menchini Puccetti, born in 1922, vividly remembers the Nazi presence. She was frequently asked to bring grapes from her family's small vineyard to the German officers.

One day, she was given two hundred lire for the grapes, and she ran all the way home to give it to her mother. "The Nazis were printing money, but it was a precious amount all the same. The officer was so kind! Then, a few days later, we heard about the *strage*, the massacre, at Sant' Anna di Stazzema, ten kilometers away, that left the entire village dead."

Signora Diana said, "We made wine with our grapes. I remember harvesting them in a heavy wooden container, the *bigoncia*, which I carried on my back. Or, we carried the grapes on our heads, balanced on the *cerdine*, a rag twisted in a circle to balance the basket better. When the wine started to ferment, the smell

would draw the partisans out of the hills, and we would give them wine and food." They saved the seeds from the pressings, and roasted and ground them to make a hot drink.

Ivano recalls the day Pietrasanta was liberated, September 19, 1944. When the church bells began pealing to announce the liberation, Ivano and many members of his family had been in hiding in a narrow space behind a wall in the cantina for five days, surviving on bread and dried chestnuts. The light of day was a most welcome sight.

Viareggio
City by the Sea

Farther down the coast of Versilia is the quaint seaside city of Viareggio, with a population of about sixty thousand. The city took a severe beating in the war, and residents had great difficulty obtaining food. Maria Aurelia Oriente (born in 1915), whose nickname is Marelia, was a young mother at the time. Her husband was a brave underwater diver for the Italian military. Left alone in her apartment in the city, she didn't have the foraging resources of those in the mountains or countryside. She did have peas. "We ate peas every day; they were part of our ration, and we had to make do with them. I invented a dish with eggs and peas, just to have something different; peas with an egg cracked in them and baked" (page 136).

If I could use only one word to describe Signora Marelia, it would be *alive*. At ninety-five, her joy in life belies the hardships she suffered: "We had nothing. No sugar, very little oil. My mother would dip the anchovies in bread crumbs twice to make them more filling for us" (page 51). Sometimes she would go out to the nearby empty lots and gather *crescione* (watercress), rosemary and other herbs, and acorns to grind for flour. With the bread provided by the rationing, she made *pancotto zuppa*: bread soaked in water and simmered with garlic, tomato, and basil. "It was *povera e buona*, both poor and good." In better times, she made *lo sfritto*, a Versilian version of *soffritto* (page 41) with *lardo* (lard) or prosciutto, garlic, onion, and sage, which she mixed in with the *minestra* (soup).

Other mainstays were salted cod and dried cod, inexpensive sources of protein; *sbroscia*, a soup made with squash and borlotti beans; and *intruglia*, a creamy corn polenta made with red beans, cavolo nero, and broth. Today, clams are called *vongole verace*, true clams, because in those days dishes were made with *vongole finte*, fake clams made with pieces of potatoes.

Isola di Capraia
Foraging the Land and the Sea

On most days, there is only one ferry from Livorno to the remote island of Capraia, located in the northern Tyrrhenian Sea, not far from Corsica. Rocky Capraia is one of the seven islands of the Tuscan Archipelago, which peaks at Cala Rossa, a 1,475-foot volcanic cone now filled with a small lake. Legend holds that when Venus came out of the sea, seven pearls came unstrung from her necklace and formed the islands. In fact, fifty thousand years ago the islands were part of the greater landmass of Italy. At the end of the Ice Age, the level of the sea rose, separating the seven high points and creating the islands of Gorgona, Capraia, Elba, Pianosa, Montecristo, Giglio, and Giannutri.

The Greeks were the first to discover the island, around 1000 B.C. They named it Aegylon, which means "place of the goats," while the name Capraia, which sounds like *capra* (goat), is derived from Latin/Etruscan *capraria*, meaning "rocky," calling up the land's volcanic origins. The Phoenicians, Etruscans, and

Romans followed with the first human settlements. The Saracen pirates that roamed the coastline and islands in search of goods and slaves challenged the early settlers. Eventually, the Romans subdued them, and in 67 B.C. assumed control of this important military and commerce stop. Even in the twentieth century, governance of the island was contested by Genoa and Pisa, with the final dominion going to Genoa, which established an agricultural penal colony that finally closed in 1986.

In 1996, the region of Tuscany designated sixty thousand hectares of the archipelago to be environmentally protected, the largest marine park in Europe. Today, Capraia has approximately 380 inhabitants living on a mere 11.4 square miles (19 square km). The oldest native resident of the island, the serene Signora Anna Bessi, was born here in 1925 and is the last person to speak the Capraian dialect. When I mentioned my interest in learning about what people ate in hard times, Signora Anna took on the same expression I had seen on others I had interviewed, a sweet, suffering look that says, "It was hard, but I am still here." She remembers well the year 1943, when no one came or went from the island. "There were mines completely surrounding the island. The Germans put them there, and we couldn't go out to fish for fear of setting one off. We lived completely off the land and the coastal fish that we could catch from the rocks, especially *totani* (squid), crab, urchins, octopus, and little mollusks."

Once covered in lush woods like the mainland, today Capraia's isolation in the salty sea has created a classic Mediterranean landscape with some oak, umbrella pines, wild oleander, and a few cork trees. The prevalent scrub is the aromatic *mirto* (myrtle), used to make a digestive liqueur, and *corbezzolo* (*Arbutus unedo*), from whose flowers a curative bitter honey is produced. Wild celery, wild artichokes, and a mythic herb called *sammule*, a wild garlic chive with a strongly pungent aroma, also grow here. The wild goats that roam the island today are called *muflone* (*Ovis musimon*), and were introduced from Sardinia and Corsica in the 1980s.

"We also set traps for wild rabbits," Signora Anna remembers of the war years, "and we had some chickens. We grew beans and *ceci* [chickpeas], and saved the seeds to replant them. We collected many kinds of greens from the *campo*, including asparagus and the wild garlic that we used in a savory cake, in fritters,

and in frittatas. Every house had a cistern to collect the rainwater for drinking and cooking, but sometimes we added seawater to give the cooked food some salty flavor."

Naturally, the recipes were simple, and Signora Anna, spry and bright at eighty-five, thinks her youthful aspect may have something to do with her natural diet. The island itself sparkles with an organic glow, and its crystalline water and pure air can only be good for the health.

After 1943, the year of solitude, commerce returned, even though there were many skirmishes between the Germans and the Americans. Sometimes, the island changed hands daily. But at least there was some access to ingredients such as flour and sugar. One of the classic Capraianese dishes, *feculina*, in fact, is a sweet cake made with potato starch, sugar, eggs, lemon zest, and vanilla powder. "It has no leavening," explains Signora Anna, "but the eggs are worked very hard—even the children had to take turns beating the eggs—and the cake rises very tall."

Today, the cuisine has evolved, as has the population. Capraia has always been frequented by ships from the mainland, bringing new ingredients and new ideas. Nearby Corsica has had a strong influence on the cuisine, and even the dialect. With two-thirds of the island protected as a national park, there won't be any danger of big changes. There is currently a small movement to bring back the more traditional dishes. The one island winery, La Piana, makes a stunning Aleatico, and another small farm produces organic honeys and jams.

Back to the mainland and heading south from Livorno, we arrive in the southern area of Tuscany called the Maremma. The Maremma exudes an untamed spirit, with its wild horses, *butteri* (cowboys), tales of pirates, flamingos, wild boar, and the amazing horned Maremmana cattle. The clustered hill towns and tiny fishing villages still seem untouched, and the seaside pristine, at least after the summer rush is over.

Pitigliano
TOLERANCE AND SURVIVAL

Arriving in Pitigliano from the coast, the first view of the hill town from the curve in the road by the sanctuary of the Madonna delle Grazie is breathtaking. The village, carved from a high outcropping of volcanic *tufo*, seems to hang suspended in an unending expanse of blue sky. Here in this southernmost part of Tuscany, Pitigliano's roots are prehistoric. It has been home, through time, to the Etruscans, Romans, and the noble Aldobrandeschi family, whose tolerance created a refuge for Jews in medieval times.

During the Renaissance, the Orsini family built a palace here, anchored by a fortress that dates back to 862. They continued the Aldobrandeschi tradition of religious tolerance, making Pitigliano and some neighboring fiefdoms havens for Jews when, in 1555, the Papal State, just across the border in Lazio, placed restrictions on them. This, along with the Inquisition in Spain, and intolerance in other areas, increased the numbers of resident Jews in Pitigliano and its surroundings. This long history of rapport between Jewish and Christian residents gave the town its nickname, Piccola Gerusalemme, or Little Jerusalem.

In 1598, a Jewish synagogue was built in Pitigliano, but within a short time, Cosimo di Medici declared further restrictions on the Jews of Florence and Siena, and restrictions were initiated here as well. Jews were forced to wear a red badge and were shut in the ghetto at night; they were also restricted from property ownership and commerce, and were subjected to high taxes.

Not until the second half of the eighteenth century were many of these restrictions lifted throughout Tuscany by the relatively liberal Grand Dukes of Tuscany, Leopoldo and Ferdinando de' Medici. This liberal atmosphere changed again in 1938, when strict racial laws, *le legge laziale*, were instituted by Mussolini, who created a number of concentration camps in Italy for political prisoners, partisans, and Jews.

At that time, one of the residents was eight-year-old Elena Servi (born in 1930). She recalls, "In 1938, my father came home one day and told me that I could no longer go to the state school. I asked him what I had done wrong. My father, with his head bowed, told me I had not done anything wrong, but I could no longer go to school."

Signora Elena remembers that many Jews left the town. "We began to feel that we were different, and rejected. It was especially difficult for my father, as he was very patriotic, decorated in the First World War." After a few years, the persecution worsened, and at the urging of their Catholic friends, Elena Servi and her family fled Pitigliano on November 11, 1943. For the next eight months, local farmers and friends sheltered them. Signora Elena remembers, "The last three months we lived in a grotto, where a farmer took us under his protection. They brought us food, and some locals even came on foot from Pitigliano to see us."

Many Jews were saved by their Christian neighbors, but at the end of the war, none remained in Pitigliano. A large group gathered in Florence, and there Signora Elena was able to resume her schooling. After she was married, she passed almost ten years in Israel, and then finally she returned to Pitigliano. Three Jews now reside in Pitigliano: Elena Servi, her son, Enrico, and her grandson, Massimo.

Among the other Pitigliano survivors was Azelio Servi, the former acting rabbi who settled in Florence after the war. He made an extraordinary effort to keep the synagogue alive, returning to hold services, until it collapsed in 1960. Azelio's daughter Edda Servi Machlin (born in 1926), moved to the United States and authored several excellent books on Italian Jewish cuisine and memories of growing up in Pitigliano. There were seven branches of the Servi family, and quite probably Azelio and Edda are distant relations of Elena Servi.

Before her family was forced into hiding, their diet was typically simple, Signora Elena reports. "Our food was Italian, with the exception of the foods for religious celebrations. Of course we didn't eat pork; we followed our dietary rules. Instead of flavoring foods with pork fat and *lardo*, we used olive oil, garlic, and onion. We ate a lot of beans and vegetables and *baccalà* [salted cod]." The Maremma is known for a simple soup called *acquacotta* (see page 64), but Signora Elena remembers her mother's *zuppa di agnello*, made with the neck bones of a lamb and vegetables and served over a slice of bread. "Sometimes my mother would put an egg in it like they do with *acquacotta*, but I didn't like the egg very much. My father hated rice because he had eaten so much of it in his military service, but he adored what he called *zuppeta*, a slice of bread covered in vegetable broth and sprinkled with sheep's milk cheese. One of my favorite dishes was *tortelli* filled with spinach and ricotta, with cheese and cinnamon on top."

Until 1939, there was a community oven that was used only once a year, during the eight days of *pesach* (Passover), when the families ate unleavened *pane azzimo*, or matzo, made with just flour and water. The women worked at a stone bench, pinching the dough to create the lattice design. "My mother was creative; one of my favorite things was when she would soak pieces of the *azzimo* in milk or water for a day, then squeeze it somewhat dry. She added a few eggs and some salt and cooked it slowly with some oil over a low flame, then sprinkled it with sugar and cinnamon." *Sfratti*, another sweet dish, was traditionally served for the Jewish New Year in Pitigliano (page 149).

Pitigliano celebrated a rebirth in 1990 when the restoration of the synagogue was completed. In 1996, Elena Servi, her sister, and her son created an association called La Piccola Gerusalemme, over which she still presides.

Florence
Victory Gardens and Rooftop Chickens

Miriam Serni Casalini (born 1928) is a poet, writer, and philosopher who grew up in Florence during the war, under circumstances much different from those who lived in the countryside. Most city people didn't have the option of foraging for food or growing their own. "We had the fortune to have family in the countryside," Signora Miriam told me. "My mother would ride eighteen kilometers and back on her bike twice a week to get bread from our family's house in Greve." The rationing was strictly controlled by the Vigili di Annona, governors of the food supply, who would stop citizens and search them. "It was risky for my mother," she remembers, "but the 150 grams of bread per person per day allowed by the rationing didn't go far. In any case, the bread they gave us was made of whole grains and seeds, heavy and dark. It might be more appreciated today, but we called it pigeon food. The *tessera/carta annonaria* [ration card] allowed a meager amount of bread, dried pasta, sugar, butter, cheese, and meat. Laborers who did heavy work got more; their *tessera* was a different color. Of course there was the black market . . ." However, black market salt

from Volterra was full of pebbles: one of Signora Miriam's jobs at home was to pick them out. Some peasant farmers came into the Sant'Ambrogio market and sold a few vegetables, and the fish seller roamed the streets carrying a giant yellow squash hollowed out and filled with fish, calling out his wares in a loud voice. She also recalls the *buzzurro* (chimney sweep) who sold polenta and *ficattole*, a fried bread snack.

Many people had *orte di guerra*, what we would call victory gardens, on the bank of the Arno River. Small pleasures included *tondone a sorpresa*, a flat bread Signora Miriam's grandmother made on top of the stove. "We had gas, but my *nonna* preferred to use coal. The *sorpresa*, or surprise, in the *tondone* was a spoonful of jam, a real treat." Signora Miriam had a neighbor with a *pollaio*, a chicken coop, on his rooftop terrace, so they were able to enjoy *frittate* often.

Meat was rare, and when it appeared it was usually a minor part of a dish. The classic Sunday lunch of *stufato*, braised or stewed meats, was a thing of the past. In fact, Signora Miriam remembers a rhyme from that time:

> *Lo stufato del Signor Pelliccia—tutti patate niente ciccia.*
> The stewed meats of Signor Pelliccia—all potatoes, no meat.

Her mother occasionally made *lesso*, boiled meats, on Sunday, and sometimes *bracciole in umido*, braised meat, but the main protein was what is called the *quinto quarto*, the fifth quarter (5/4), or offal. After the animal is quartered, these are the parts that remain: stomach, lungs, organs, and even the udder. Prepared properly, these meats are delicious. (See page 109 for *Trippa alla Fiorentina*.)

Even in Florence, chestnuts figured prominently in the diet. The local *rosticceria* had *castagnaccio* (page 155), polenta *dolce*, and *necci* (page 58), all made with chestnut flour and water, with very little sugar, due to the sweetness of the chestnut flour. Signora Miriam's favorite was *pattona*, a cross between *castagnaccio* and *necci*, topped with ricotta cheese. Even better were the carts at Carnevale, with *schiacciata* (a thin focaccia), *bruscolata* (salted pumpkin seeds), and *lupini*, large, yellow protein-rich legumes that lost favor after the war, as they really were associated with animal feed. Now, you often see them in markets next to candies and roasted nuts.

Rebuilding and Reeducation

The end of the war was a relief, but it left behind major destruction and the need to rebuild not only buildings and infrastructures, but also the society itself. Under the Truman Doctrine, a number of humanitarian and relief efforts were funded by the United States, one of which was the Marshall Plan, also known as the European Recovery Program. In a speech given by George Marshall in 1947, he said, "It is logical that the United States should do whatever it is able to do to assist in the return of normal economic health to the world, without which there can be no political stability and no assured peace. Our policy is not directed against any country, but against hunger, poverty, desperation and chaos." Critics claim it was a move to fight communism, but regardless of the viewpoint, help was desperately needed and provided. The idea was to

strengthen individual countries under their own governance. Grants and loans were given to industries to provide jobs, and other moneys went to agricultural rehabilitation, education, medical and sanitation needs, and to provide the basics of food and clothing to devastated countries.

Dr. Evelina Modigliani Rossi, born in 1917, created and managed one such program in Italy from 1950 to 1973. Having already earned a doctorate in agriculture at the Giuseppina Alfieri Cavour Women's Farming and Domestic Science Institute, Signora Evelina recalls, "I replaced my father, who was serving in the war, as assistant professor at the Institute of Agronomy in Florence. I was very pleased when I was selected to administer a new program funded by the Marshall Plan to educate rural women.

"Many people have the misconception that all peasant women were expert at managing a household, preserving foods, and dealing with domestic medical situations. The fact is that life spans were shortened drastically by a lack of such knowledge, particularly with regard to sanitation and diet," she explains. At the turn of the century, there were few schools for women, and most were not in the rural areas, which sorely needed them. Education under early Fascist rule had suffered, except education for the privileged. Some programs slowly grew outside the public school sector, led by traveling lecturers teaching new agricultural techniques, but these were designed for boys and young men.

By the early 1930s, the Fascists assigned itinerant educators to provide training in agricultural and domestic skills for rural women, with the goal of keeping families on the farm rather than moving to urban and industrial areas. Techniques such as beekeeping, animal husbandry, and silk farming were taught, with the goal of making women more efficient at home while not threatening the livelihood of men. The Fascist propaganda of the time celebrated women as "mothers of the nation and guardians of the rural world," but they were, in fact, overworked and quite poor. World War II did not improve the situation.

Signora Evelina describes her rural education program: "We selected thirty women from deprived areas, brought them to Florence for a nine-month residential program, and then sent them home to share what they had learned with their peers. Under the Marshall Plan, I was brought to the United States for three months to study with home demonstration agents," a program begun in the early 1900s in the States to help educate people on the farm. The program disseminated information about preserving foods through brining, canning, drying, and curing. Later, subjects such as sewing, nutrition, sanitation, and home nursing were introduced. Signora Evelina explains, "In Italy, the same program was used as a model to teach women horticulture, agriculture, healthful eating, first aid, food preservation, and the care of children."

Montepulciano
Back Home in the Tuscan Hills

At my table, Virio says, "If my mother could see this meal, how I live, she wouldn't believe it. Heat in every room. Running water, a soft bed, and all of this good food."

Even when we experience changes in our lives with fluctuating economies and priorities, it's important to remember how good our lives are, and to reflect on the simple pleasures.

One thing that impressed me about almost every person that I interviewed for this book was that even though they had lived through difficult times and sometimes unimaginable experiences, they remain positive and appreciative of the smallest things in their lives today.

Take joy in small pleasures and eat well.

The Recipes

Italy is made up of twenty regions that have been united for only the past 150 years. Each region has maintained a unique cultural and agricultural identity based on a specific climate, geography, economy, and history of foreign influence. Even within one region, especially one as large as Tuscany, there are many variations on a theme. When these recipes originated, travel between communities was limited, and dishes were developed largely in isolation. A dish from two different areas can have the same name, but be prepared in a very different way, or the same recipe may also have a different name. *Farinata*, for example, can be made with different flours (corn, chickpea, wheat, and so on), and it can be prepared in diverse modes. In Liguria, it is a thin cake made with chickpea flour and baked in a wood-burning oven; in Tuscany, that same dish is called *cecina*, or sometimes *torta di ceci* (chickpea cake). In the recipe on page 68, it is a soup thickened with flour—in this case—corn flour.

Within a village there can be as many variations as there are cooks. *Pappa al pomodoro* (page 66) is a good example. It is basically bread and tomatoes; however, one person toasts the bread and another uses dry bread. One crumbles the bread or uses bread crumbs, another chunks it, and someone else slices. For some people, it's an after-school snack; for others, it's a whole meal. I have selected my favorite way to make a recipe; you should adjust it and make it your own as well.

The bread used in these recipes should ideally be wood-fired saltless bread. Since that is hard to find outside Tuscany, I've given a recipe (page 147), but you can also use a country-style bread from your market or baker.

Appetizers were not necessarily part of the peasant table. What we enjoy as an appetizer today might have sufficed for an entire meal in the past. A crust of leftover bread was often topped with a salted anchovy or, as many people told me, the anchovy was passed around the table for each person to rub the bread with it for a bit of aroma. There is a phrase, *pane e companatico*, that means "bread and something to go with the bread." Sometimes that "something" was more bread.

In the past, except for special occasions, meat was considered a condiment rather than a main course, and was used to flavor pastas, rice, or soups. The main focus was on grains and seasonal vegetables that could be cultivated or foraged. Soups and pastas were a means of using up leftover bits of food. When there was time, or the means to obtain it, game was part of the fare. Apart from the season when the animals were butchered, fresh pork and beef were rarely seen on the table. I have included several meat dishes because we have more access to meats, but also to illustrate how cooking methods can transform an economical cut of meat into something delectable.

Desserts were relegated to special occasions. Sugar was expensive, so any daily sweet was fruit or jams made from fruit. This may be one of the reasons Tuscany is not known for elaborate desserts. On holy days and for birthdays, the favorites were *ciambellone* (page 156), a simple cake; *panforte* and *panettone*; and a variety of cookies. Each area has a special cookie: Pisa makes the wafer-like *brigidini*, first created by nuns; from Prato come the *cantucci*, or *biscotti di Prato*; and in Siena, you find *cavallucci* and *ricciarelli* (recipes on pages 166 and 164). Most of these cookies are quite hard and dry so that they will keep for a while; a nice glass of vin santo (sweet wine) or *vin brulé* (warmed wine) is perfect for dipping and softening them.

In any case, the following recipes are descendants of harder times. Now we have access to the basic ingredients that then were not always available, so I have updated the recipes to reflect that. We may use stock or wine instead of water for cooking, we can use more meat and a greater range of vegetables, and we probably have fewer people to feed, so our portion sizes are larger. The principles of an economic and flavorful kitchen are the same, however, starting with food in season.

Today, we see a renewed interest in seasonal and local foods, an ancient concept that is the basis of peasant cuisine. Eating foods produced close to home supports local farmers and producers, and lessens the economic and environmental impact of transporting food.

I hope that the recipes in this book, which were born in frugality and innovation, will help you to make use of your own local foods in season, allowing these ancient dishes to live again in your own kitchen.

Erbe e Soffritto: Seasonings

Tuscan cooks have two fundamental seasonings: erbe aromatiche al sale, aromatic herbs with salt, and the vegetable mixture soffritto. Both mixtures are traditionally minced using a mezzaluna, a half-moon-shaped double knife.

Erbe Aromatiche al Sale: Aromatic Herbs Minced with Salt

This handy blend sits by most Tuscan stoves, ready to be sprinkled over a roast or grilled vegetables, or to season a sauce. Each cook has his or her own combination of flavors: rosemary, thyme, parsley, and sage are some favorites. A handful of fresh herbs are minced with an equal amount of salt. The salt adds flavor, but it also draws the essential oils that are left on the cutting board back into the mixture. This blend is wonderful used fresh but will keep for several days; the salt preserves the herbs, drying them and concentrating the flavor.

Soffritto: Carrot, Celery, and Onion Foundation

I call soffritto the holy trinity of the Tuscan kitchen, a finely chopped mixture of equal parts carrot, celery, and onion (the aromatic vegetables, or odori) that is cooked until golden in olive oil to become the foundation of most soups, sauces, and stews. As the onion cooks, the sugars start to caramelize, the carrot sweetens, and the celery releases its unique flavor. Cooks may have their own variations according to local tradition and personal choice; some may add pancetta or lardo, or vary the proportions of the vegetables.

Per capire una cosa,
devi guardare alle radici.

To understand something, you must look at its roots.

Appetizers

AFFETTATI   44
Sliced Cured Meats

BRUSCHETTA AL POMODORO   47
Toasted Bread with Tomato

PAN' SANTO   48
Holy Bread

CROSTINI DEL CORTILE   49
Farmyard Crostini

FIORI DI ZUCCHINE   50
Stuffed Zucchini Flowers

ACCIUGHE FRITTE   51
Fried Anchovies

FRITTURA MISTA DI VERDURE   53
Fried Flowers and Vegetables

PINZIMONIO   54
Crudités with Olive Oil

FRITTATA CON CICORIA   57
Eggs with Wild Greens

NECCI   58
Chestnut Crêpes

Affettati
SLICED CURED MEATS

In times of no refrigeration, cured meats were an important source of protein, enabling the family to preserve the meat after an animal was butchered. Sliced cured meats often sufficed for a whole meal, especially on days when there was work to be done. Seasonal accompaniments might include fresh fruit, olives, or nuts.

6 thin slices pancetta

6 thin slices prosciutto di Parma

12 slices *finocchiona* salame
  (Tuscan-style salame with fennel seeds
  or your favorite salame)

Sliced country-style bread or *grissini*
  (bread sticks)

Arrange the meats on a cutting board or serving platter. Accompany with a basket of bread.

SERVES 4

Bruschetta al Pomodoro

TOASTED BREAD WITH TOMATO

Bruschetta literally means "toasted," and a slice of grilled or toasted bread can be served with many different toppings. Traditionally, the first pressing of the olive harvest is tasted on the spot and drizzled over bruschetta, which is also called fettunta.

1 loaf country-style bread (1 pound), sliced 1/2 inch thick

2 cloves garlic

2 tomatoes, diced

A few fresh basil leaves, torn into small pieces

3 tablespoons extra-virgin olive oil, plus more for drizzling

Sea salt

Grill or toast the bread on both sides. Remove from the heat and immediately rub with the cloves of garlic. In a medium bowl, combine the tomatoes, basil, the 3 tablespoons olive oil, and salt to taste. Spoon the tomato mixture onto the bread, place on a serving platter, and drizzle with olive oil.

SERVES 6

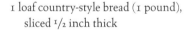

Clockwise from bottom, center: Bruschetta al Pomodoro, Pan' Santo, and Crostini del Cortile

Pan' Santo

Holy Bread

Cavolo nero, literally "black cabbage," is a dark, leafy vegetable grown in the late fall and winter, best after the first frost. In the United States, it is known as dinosaur or lacinato kale. If you are unable to find it in your market, substitute regular kale, Swiss chard, or spinach and decrease the cooking time by half. I imagine this is called "holy bread" because it is "anointed" with liquid.

1/4 cup extra-virgin olive oil, plus more for drizzling

1 onion, finely chopped

3 ounces pancetta, finely chopped

1 dried *peperoncino* (dried red pepper) or pinch of red pepper flakes (optional)

20 leaves cavolo nero, julienned

1 cup vegetable, meat, or chicken stock (page 172 or 173)

Sea salt and freshly ground black pepper

6 slices country-style bread

1 clove garlic

In a large sauté pan, heat the 1/4 cup olive oil over medium heat and sauté the onion, pancetta, and *peperoncino* until the onion is golden, about 5 minutes. Remove the *peperoncino* and discard. Add the cavolo nero and stock; cover and simmer for 20 to 30 minutes, or until the cavolo nero is softened. Uncover and simmer another 10 minutes to reduce the cooking liquid. Season with salt and pepper to taste, and remove from the heat.

Toast the bread and rub it with the garlic clove. Arrange the toasts on a tray and top with the cavolo nero mixture. Drizzle with olive oil and serve at once.

SERVES 6

Crostini del Cortile

FARMYARD CROSTINI

In a culture where nothing is wasted, all parts of the animals are used. Chickens, geese, and ducks ranged freely in the farmyard. When one of these birds was butchered, the innards were used to make a delicious mixture to spread on a slice of bread. My friend Lina Mazzetti taught me to add a bit of apple and anchovy to round out the flavor.

2 tablespoons extra-virgin olive oil

1/2 onion, finely chopped

6 ounces chicken, goose, or duck giblets (livers, heart, and gizzards)

1 apple, peeled, cored, and diced

1/4 cup dry white wine or vin santo

1/2 cup chicken stock (page 173)

1 anchovy fillet

1/2 teaspoon minced fresh thyme

1 tablespoon minced fresh flat-leaf parsley

1 tablespoon salt-cured capers, rinsed

Sea salt and freshly ground black pepper

12 slices country-style bread, toasted

In a medium skillet, heat the olive oil over medium heat and sauté the onion for about 3 minutes, or until translucent. Add the giblets and apple and cook for 4 to 5 minutes, or until the onion is browned and the giblets are crisp. Add the wine and stir to scrape up the browned bits from the bottom of the pan. Add the chicken stock and anchovy and cook for 10 to 12 minutes, or until the giblets are firm to the touch and the mixture has thickened. Transfer to a food processor and pureé until smooth. Stir in the thyme, parsley, capers, and salt and pepper to taste. Set aside and let cool.

To serve, spread a thin layer of the paste onto the toasted bread and arrange on a platter.

SERVES 6

Fiori di Zucchine

STUFFED ZUCCHINI FLOWERS

Early summer is announced by the call of the cuckoo birds and the first zucchini flowers. Each plant bears both male and female flowers; the short-stemmed female flower bears the fruit. The longer-stemmed male flowers, the pollinators, are harvested for frying, but flowers with baby zucchini attached can also be used.

12 very fresh zucchini flowers

1 cup (8 ounces) whole-milk ricotta

1 teaspoon minced fresh thyme

1 teaspoon minced fresh basil

3 tablespoons grated pecorino cheese

Sea salt

Extra-virgin olive oil for drizzling

Freshly ground black pepper

Preheat the oven to 350°F. Lightly oil a baking sheet.

Carefully rinse the zucchini flowers and remove the stamens. Blanch the flowers in boiling water for 3 seconds. Using a wire skimmer or slotted spoon, immediately transfer to a bowl of ice water for a few seconds to stop the cooking process. Using a wire skimmer or slotted spoon, immediately transfer to paper towels to drain.

In a medium bowl, combine the ricotta, herbs, and pecorino. Stir to blend, and then season to taste with salt. Fit a pastry bag with a large, plain tip. Fill with the mixture and squeeze some gently into each open flower until full. Twist the ends closed and place on the prepared pan.

Drizzle with olive oil, season with salt and pepper to taste, and bake for 4 to 6 minutes, or until heated through. Transfer to a serving platter and serve at once.

SERVES 6

Acciughe Fritte

FRIED ANCHOVIES

Maria Aurelia Oriente (see page 24) remembers these delicacies, made by her mother. To make the morsels go further, her mother battered and coated the anchovies twice. Fresh anchovies are delicious and full of good nutrition, but if they are unavailable, use salt-cured ones instead. Rinse the anchovies and press one on a sage leaf, smearing it to make it stick, then continue with the batter and fry as indicated below.

1 pound fresh anchovies, butterflied, cleaned, and heads removed (tails intact)

2 large eggs

1 teaspoon minced fresh marjoram

Sea salt and freshly ground black pepper

Canola oil for deep-frying

20 to 25 fresh sage leaves

1/2 to 3/4 cup fine dried bread crumbs

Rinse and drain the anchovies.

In a small bowl, beat the eggs with the marjoram and a pinch of salt and pepper. Place the bread crumbs in another bowl.

In a medium saucepan, heat 3 inches of oil to 375°F on a deep-fat thermometer.

Place a sage leaf on each anchovy and dip it in the egg mixture, then the bread crumbs. Press lightly to attach the coating to the anchovies, and dip each again in the egg and crumbs a second time. Add the coated anchovies carefully to the hot oil, and cook for 1 to 2 minutes on each side. Using a wire skimmer or a slotted spoon, transfer to paper towels to drain. Sprinkle with salt and serve at once.

SERVES 4

Frittura Mista di Verdure

FRIED FLOWERS AND VEGETABLES

I make this appetizer year-round. In the fall and winter, I use strips of winter squash, sage, and sliced potatoes; in the spring, elderberry and acacia flowers; and in summer, zucchini flowers and eggplant. The important thing is to heat the oil to a temperature of 375°F; at this point, less oil is absorbed by the food. Fry in small batches, as large quantities will decrease the temperature of the oil.

2 large eggs

3 tablespoons sparkling water, beer, or Prosecco

1 teaspoon sea salt, plus more for sprinkling

1/4 cup unbleached all-purpose flour

Sunflower oil for frying

8 zucchini flowers (or your local edible flower), rinsed and patted dry

1 zucchini, cut into sticks

1 small onion, sliced and separated into rings

In a small bowl, combine the eggs, sparkling water, and the 1 teaspoon salt. Whisk in the flour until the mixture is smooth and the consistency of pancake batter.

In a heavy, medium saucepan, heat 2 inches of oil to 375°F on a deep-fat thermometer. Working in batches, dip the flowers and prepared vegetables in the batter and fry for 2 minutes, then turn and fry for another 2 minutes, or until golden brown. Using a wire skimmer or a slotted spoon, transfer to paper towels to drain. Sprinkle with salt and serve at once.

SERVES 4

Pinzimonio

CRUDITÉS WITH OLIVE OIL

Italian-style restaurants in America often put a plate of olive oil on the table for guests to dip their bread into. But that just doesn't happen in Italy. This recipe for a seasoned oil to dip vegetables in is the closest you will get to that idea. Use seasonal vegetables: In the spring and summer, take advantage of tender peas, asparagus, baby carrots, fennel, and sweet bell peppers. In fall and winter, choose more robust vegetables, such as cardoons, mushrooms, potatoes, and roasted beets.

4 ounces broccoli florets, blanched

4 ounces cauliflower florets, blanched

4 ounces asparagus, trimmed to 4-inch lengths and blanched

3 carrots, peeled and cut into 4-inch-long strips

1 fennel bulb, cored and cut into wedges

2 red bell peppers, seeded, deveined, and cut into 4-inch-long strips

1 1/2 cups extra-virgin olive oil

Sea salt and freshly ground black pepper

Arrange the vegetables on a platter. Offer your guests extra-virgin olive oil in individual dipping bowls, and let them season it to taste with salt and pepper.

SERVES 6

Frittata con Cicoria

Eggs with Wild Greens

Arugula is a good substitute for dandelion greens in this frittata. Adding leftover pasta or potatoes to the eggs before cooking makes for a more substantial dish.

3 tablespoons extra-virgin olive oil

1 medium onion, finely chopped

4 ounces dandelion greens or arugula leaves, julienned

6 large eggs

Sea salt and freshly ground black pepper

In a 10-inch nonstick skillet, heat 2 tablespoons of the olive oil over medium heat, and sauté the onion and greens for 3 to 4 minutes, or until the onion is translucent and greens have wilted. Remove from the heat.

In a medium bowl, beat the eggs until blended, and season with salt and pepper to taste. Add the cooked onion mixture.

Heat the remaining 1 tablespoon olive oil in the same sauté pan. Add the egg mixture and cook, stirring gently, for 3 to 4 minutes, or until the eggs have set. Loosen the edges, flip the frittata over by sliding it onto a plate, then reverse it into the pan and cook the second side for 2 to 3 minutes, or until golden. Cut into fourths and serve at once.

Serves 4

Necci

Chestnut Crêpes

Signora Eni Fiorini Marcucci (see page 16) uses ancient stones to make these crêpes in her fireplace. This recipe has been adapted for the modern kitchen. The traditional filling is fresh sheep's milk ricotta, but cooked beans (page 133), onion frittata, sautéed wild greens, or bits of leftover roasted meat can also be used. The crêpes can also be drizzled with chestnut honey and served as a dessert.

2¹/₂ cups chestnut flour

2 cups spring water

¹/₂ teaspoon sea salt

Piece of pork rind or cooking oil to grease cooking surface

1 cup (8 ounces) whole-milk ricotta, preferably sheep's milk

In a large bowl, whisk the flour, salt, and water together until smooth. Cover and set aside for at least 1 hour or as long as overnight.

Heat a 7-inch nonstick crêpe pan or skillet over medium heat. Smear the pan with the pork rind (or brush with oil). Stir the batter and pour a scant ¹/₄ cup into the pan. Tilt the pan so that the batter runs to the edges, creating a thin, even layer. Immediately loosen the edges with a spatula and cook for 1 minute, or until the top is set and looks dry. Turn and cook for 15 to 30 seconds, just to lightly brown the bottom. Stack the crêpes with parchment paper between them to keep the crêpes from sticking to one another until ready to use. Repeat for each crêpe, greasing the pan lightly each time before adding the batter.

To serve, place a tablespoonful of ricotta on each crêpe and roll it up. Serve at once.

Makes 12 crêpes; serves 6

Chi vuol vivere serenamente,
viva sobrio e allegramente.

Whoever wants a serene life, should live a humble and happy life.

Soups

Garmugia Lucchese
LUCCA'S SPRING VEGETABLE SOUP

*The origins of this soup go back to the 1600s.
It is another version of a seasonal soup that uses
whatever vegetables are at hand. In this case, it
is a spring soup of early vegetables: asparagus,
fava beans, fresh peas, and artichokes, flavored
with small amounts of pancetta and veal.*

3 tablespoons extra-virgin olive oil

2 ounces pancetta, diced

2 ounces ground veal

4 spring onions or green onions,
   sliced crosswise

4 baby artichokes, trimmed and thinly sliced

4 baby carrots, peeled and cut into thin rounds

4 stalks asparagus, trimmed and cut into
   ^{1}/$_2$-inch lengths

^{1}/$_4$ cup green peas

4 ounces fava beans in the pod, shelled,
   blanched for 1 minute, and peeled

4 cups chicken stock (page 173), heated

Sea salt and freshly ground black pepper

4 slices country-style bread, toasted

In a large, heavy saucepan, heat the olive oil over
medium heat, and add the pancetta, veal, and onions.
Cook, stirring, for 4 to 5 minutes, or until the veal has
browned. Add the artichokes and carrots, and cook
until softened, about 2 minutes. Add the asparagus,
peas, and fava beans, and cook for 2 minutes. Add the
chicken stock, bring to a boil, decrease the heat to a
simmer, and cook, uncovered, for 30 minutes. Season
with salt and pepper to taste.

Place a slice of toasted bread in each of 4 shallow soup
bowls and ladle the soup over it. Serve at once.

SERVES 4

Acquacotta

BREAD, ONION, AND GREENS SOUP

The word acquacotta literally means "cooked water,"
and this soup is a traditional dish from the southern
coastal part of Tuscany known as the Maremma.
Because meat was rare and often the only liquid
available was water, this was a kind of "stone soup"
to which leftover bits of other foods were added.

$^{\text{I}}\!/_2$ cup extra-virgin olive oil

1 onion, finely chopped

2 carrots, peeled and finely chopped

1 stalk celery, finely chopped

Pinch of red pepper flakes

1 pound chard or spinach, steamed (page 175)
   and coarsely chopped

1 pound ripe tomatoes, peeled, seeded, and
   coarsely chopped (page 175)

6 cups water

Sea salt and freshly ground pepper

6 large eggs

$^{\text{I}}\!/_2$ teaspoon white wine vinegar

6 thin slices country-style bread, toasted

In a large saucepan, heat the olive oil over medium
heat. Add the onion, carrots, celery, and pepper flakes.
Cook for 4 to 5 minutes, or until the onion is golden,
then add the chard. Cover, decrease the heat to low,
and cook for 10 minutes. Add the tomatoes and water.
Bring to a boil, decrease the heat to a simmer, cover,
and cook for 45 minutes. Season with salt and pepper.

Meanwhile, poach the eggs. Bring a large saucepan
of water to a boil, add the vinegar and a pinch of salt,
then decrease the heat to a high simmer. Crack an egg
into a soup ladle, then slide it into the water. Repeat
with the remaining five eggs, cooking the eggs for
3 minutes, or until the white has set.

Place a slice of toasted bread in each of 6 shallow
soup bowls. Using a slotted spoon, transfer each egg
to each slice of toasted bread. Bring the soup to the
table, stir it well, and ladle it into each bowl over the
egg and serve at once.

SERVES 6

Zuppa di Farro
Farro Soup

Farro (Triticum dicoccum), *also sometimes called emmer, is an ancient strain of wheat thought to be one of the oldest grains in the Mediterranean. Found in Italy since Roman times, it was replaced for awhile with higher-producing types of wheat, but has made a comeback due to its nutty flavor, chewy texture, and because it is a good source of protein.*

1/4 cup extra-virgin olive oil, plus more
   for drizzling

1 medium onion, finely chopped

1 large carrot, peeled and finely chopped

1 stalk celery, finely chopped

2 cloves garlic, minced

2 cups whole farro

6 cups vegetable or chicken stock
   (page 172 or 173), heated

1/2 cup cooked cannellini beans (page 133)

Sea salt and freshly ground black pepper

1/4 cup minced fresh flat-leaf parsley

In a medium soup pot, heat the 1/4 cup olive oil over medium heat, and sauté the onion, carrot, and celery for 4 to 5 minutes, or until the onion is golden. Add the garlic and farro, and stir for 2 minutes. Gradually stir in the stock, allowing the farro to absorb some of the liquid. Cook, stirring frequently, for about 30 minutes, or until the farro is tender.

In a blender, purée half of the beans; add the puréed and whole beans to the soup and heat through. Season with salt and pepper to taste. Serve in warmed soup bowls, garnished with parsley and a drizzle of olive oil.

Serves 4

Pappa al Pomodoro
TOMATO-BREAD SOUP

This was the classic after-school snack in the past. Still pleasing to all ages, it can be made with fresh tomatoes in season, or with canned tomatoes in the off season. The word pappa *means "baby food" or "mush," giving you a clue to the consistency of this soup. It was another of the many ways to use dry, day-old bread. If you don't want to make the traditional unsalted bread on page 147, use your favorite country-style bread and toast it.*

1/2 cup extra-virgin olive oil

3 cloves garlic, halved, plus 1 whole clove garlic

Pinch of red pepper flakes

1 pound fresh tomatoes, peeled, seeded, and cubed (see page 175), or 1 (14 1/2-ounce) can peeled whole Italian tomatoes with juice, coarsely chopped

4 slices country-style bread, toasted

3 cups vegetable stock (page 172)

Sea salt and freshly ground black pepper

1/4 cup fresh basil leaves, julienned

In heavy, medium saucepan, combine the oil, halved garlic cloves, and pepper flakes, and cook over low heat for about 5 minutes to infuse the oil with the flavors; don't let the garlic burn. Using a slotted spoon, remove the garlic and discard. Add the tomatoes and simmer for 15 minutes.

Rub the toasted bread with the whole garlic clove, and place the bread in a large heatproof casserole. Pour the vegetable stock, and then the tomato mixture over the toast, and cook over medium-high heat for 10 minutes. Season with salt and pepper to taste. Spoon into warmed soup bowls and garnish with the basil.

SERVES 4

Farinata Toscana
TUSCAN CORNMEAL, KALE, AND BEAN SOUP

This recipe is from food historian Nancy Harmon Jenkins' book Flavors of Tuscany. The origins of the soup are in the Casentino Mountains above Arezzo. In hard times, it could have been made with any kind of flour and foraged wild greens or mushrooms. It may be eaten as a thick soup, but like polenta, it is sometimes spread on a board to firm up, then sliced and fried in olive oil.

$^{1}/_{2}$ cup dried cannellini beans, rinsed and picked over

1 (6-inch) strip fresh pork rind, or 2 tablespoons extra-virgin olive oil

1 small bunch kale or cavolo nero (dinosaur or lacinato kale)

2 ounces pancetta, chopped

$^{1}/_{2}$ medium onion

1 stalk celery

1 carrot, peeled

$^{1}/_{2}$ cup fresh flat-leaf parsley leaves

1 clove garlic, crushed

2 tablespoons fresh rosemary leaves

2 tablespoons extra-virgin olive oil, plus more for drizzling

2 medium potatoes, peeled and cubed

$^{1}/_{2}$ teaspoon fennel seeds, crushed

Sea salt

3$^{1}/_{2}$ cups water

1 cup coarsely ground cornmeal or polenta

8 thin slices country-style bread, toasted or fried in extra-virgin olive oil

Grated aged pecorino or Parmigiano-Reggiano cheese for garnish

Place the beans in a medium saucepan with water to cover by 2 inches; soak overnight.

Drain the beans and place them in a small saucepan with the pork rind or olive oil. Add water to cover by 1 inch. Bring to a boil, decrease the heat, cover, and simmer for 1 1/2 hours, or until the beans are tender but not falling apart, adding a little boiling water from time to time if necessary. Remove the pork rind and discard. Set the beans aside in their cooking liquid.

Remove and discard the tough central ribs from the kale. Stack and roll the leaves into a cylinder, then cut them into shreds crosswise. You should have about 4 cups, tightly packed. Rinse the leaves well but do not dry. Set aside.

On a cutting board, chop together the pancetta, onion, celery, carrot, parsley, garlic, and rosemary until the mixture is very fine.

In a soup kettle, heat the 2 tablespoons olive oil over medium heat and sauté the chopped mixture for 4 to 5 minutes, or until the vegetables are soft but not brown. Add the cooked beans and all their liquid and stir to mix well. Add the shredded kale, the potatoes, fennel seeds, and salt to taste. Add 1 1/2 cups of the water and bring to a boil. Decrease the heat to a simmer and cook for about 20 minutes, or until the potatoes are cooked through and the other vegetables are very soft. The *farinata* may be prepared ahead of time up to this point. When ready to continue, heat the vegetable mixture to simmering, adding a little more water if necessary.

In a medium bowl, combine the cornmeal and the remaining 2 cups water. Stir until the cornmeal has absorbed the water, then gradually stir the cornmeal into the simmering soup until blended. Cook, stirring frequently, for 40 minutes, to make a very thick, porridgy soup.

Spoon the *farinata* over the toasted or fried bread. Drizzle with olive oil and sprinkle with a little grated cheese. Serve at once.

Serves 8

Ribollita
CLASSIC TUSCAN VEGETABLE-BREAD SOUP

The restaurant Da Delfina in Artimino, just west of Florence, is a reference point for cucina povera. Chef Carlo Cioni understands intimately the relationship between the land and the table. In his hands, a sturdy vegetable soup is transformed into a second dish by layering leftover soup with bread, then into a third dish by baking the leftover layered soup and bread. The fourth and final transformation is ribollita, the remaining vegetable stew cooked in a skillet, a dish that exemplifies the resourcefulness of Tuscan cooks.

Carlo insists it must be made on top of the stove, not in the oven, a version often seen in restaurants. Oil is used sparingly for this is a peasant dish. The ingredients vary according to what is available, but Carlo explains, "There must be a balance between the dolce (sweet), aromatica (aromatic), and amaro (bitter)." The sweet is found in herbs, such as parsley, celery, and purslane; the aromatic is in thyme, borage, and fennel; and the bitter essences come from mustard greens and chicory. A leafy green is always present; in the winter, cavolo nero, and in the summer, cabbage.

Carlo admonishes cooks to handle the beans tenderly and cook them slowly, and "dolcemente," gently, so they are not broken or crushed. He soaks them overnight with aromatics: whole cloves of garlic, a bay leaf, and a sprig of sage. Use any seasonal vegetables in this soup, and cook them in the order of hardness; start with vegetables such as potatoes that take longer to cook, and finish with the tender herbs.

(recipe continued on page 73)

Ribollita (continued)

2 tablespoons extra-virgin olive oil,
  plus more for drizzling

1 onion, finely chopped, plus ¹/₂ cup more
  chopped onion for Day 3

2 carrots, peeled and finely chopped

1 stalk celery, finely chopped

2 cloves garlic, minced

10 cups vegetable stock (page 172)

1 or 2 boiling potatoes, peeled and cubed

3 zucchini, coarsely chopped

4 cups shredded cavolo nero (dinosaur or
  lacinato kale) or regular kale

1 cup shredded assorted leafy greens (such as
  Swiss chard, nettles, and spinach)

1 cup coarsely chopped aromatic greens
  (such as borage, fennel, and mustard)

2 cups cooked cannellini beans (page 133)

¹/₄ cup minced mixed aromatic herbs
  (such as fresh flat-leaf parsley, rosemary,
  and sage)

Sea salt and freshly ground black pepper

1 pound day-old country bread, thinly sliced

DAY 1: MINESTRA DI VERDURA (*Vegetable Soup*)
In a large soup pot, heat the oil over medium heat and sauté the onion, carrots, and celery for 4 to 5 minutes, or until the onion is golden. Add the garlic and stock, stirring to scrape up the browned bits from the bottom of the pan. Increase the heat to medium-high and add the potatoes and zucchini. Cook for 10 minutes, then add the cavolo nero and leafy greens. Decrease the temperature to a simmer and cook for 20 minutes. Add the beans and aromatic herbs. Simmer for 10 minutes to heat the beans through. Season to taste with salt and pepper. Serve in warmed soup bowls.

SERVES 8

DAY 2: MINESTRA DI PANE (*Bread Soup*)
In a saucepan, warm the leftover soup over medium-low heat. Place very thin slices of country-style bread in the bottom of a lightly oiled baking dish. Spoon one-third of the hot soup over the bread, and repeat with two more layers of bread and soup. Cover and let stand for 15 minutes to 1 hour in a warm place before serving.

DAY 3: MINESTRA DI PANE AL FORNO (*Baked Bread Soup*)
In a preheated 375°F oven, heat the leftover Bread Soup in its baking dish. Sprinkle with chopped onion and drizzle with olive oil. Return to the oven and bake for 20 minutes, or until the onions are lightly browned.

DAY 4: RIBOLLITA (*Recooked Vegetable Stew*)
Lightly brush a medium skillet with olive oil. Spoon the remaining Baked Bread Soup into the pan and brown over medium heat for 4 to 5 minutes, or until crisp on the bottom. Turn and cook for about 4 to 5 minutes to crisp the second side. Drizzle lightly with olive oil and sprinkle with freshly ground black pepper. The *ribollita* should be firm enough to eat with a fork. Serve at once.

Carabaccia

Onion Soup

Sweet, tender onions, bread, and cheese—this is comfort food. The recipe for this Florentine dish goes back to the Renaissance, and many believe it to be the forerunner of French onion soup.

1/2 cup extra-virgin olive oil

2 pounds sweet red onions, very thinly sliced

6 cups meat stock (page 172), heated

Sea salt and freshly ground black pepper

4 slices country-style bread, toasted

2 1/2 cups coarsely grated pecorino or
    Parmigiano-Reggiano cheese

In a large soup pot, heat the olive oil over low heat. Add the onions and cook, stirring occasionally, for 20 to 30 minutes, or until the onions are caramelized. Add the stock, cover, and simmer for another 30 minutes. Season to taste with salt and pepper.

Preheat the oven to 400°F. Place a slice of toasted bread in each of 4 individual ovenproof soup bowls. Divide the onion soup among the bowls, and sprinkle one-fourth of the cheese into each bowl. Bake for 5 minutes, or until the cheese has melted and formed a crust.

Serves 4

*I mugnai so' l'ultimi
a mori di fame.*

The miller is the last to die of hunger.

Pastas & Grains

INSALATA DI FARRO 78
Farro Salad

PANZANELLA 81
Bread Salad

POLENTA DI CASTAGNA CON
SALSICCE 82
Chestnut Polenta with Fresh Sausage

POLENTA DI MAIS DI OTTO FILE 85
Corn Polenta

PICI ALL'AGLIONE 87
Pasta with Garlic-Tomato Sauce

TAGLIATELLE AL RAGÙ DI DOMENICA 88
Tagliatelle with Sunday Meat Sauce

PASTA AL FORNO 89
Baked Pasta

GNUDI 90
Spinach and Ricotta Dumplings

PASTA ALLE BRICIOLE 93
Pasta with Spicy Bread Crumb Topping

PENNE AL SUGO DI LEPRE 94
Pasta with Wild Hare or Rabbit Sauce

TORTELLI DI PATATE DEL MUGELLO
CON BURRO FUSO E SALVIA 96
*Tortelli with Potato Filling
and Melted Butter and Sage*

Insalata di Farro

FARRO SALAD

*Farro is an ancient strain of wheat with a high
protein content and a nutty flavor. It can be found in
natural foods and gourmet foods stores whole, cracked,
or ground into flour. This dish can be served warm as
a winter side dish, or chilled for a summer salad.*

2 cups whole-grain farro

3 tablespoons plus ¹/₄ cup extra-virgin olive oil

4 green onions, including 1 inch of green parts,
   chopped

2 cloves garlic, minced

1 zucchini, diced

1 red bell pepper, seeded, deveined, and diced

2 cups chicken stock (page 173), heated

1 cup canned chickpeas, drained and rinsed

4 ounces spicy salame, diced

Grated zest and juice of ¹/₂ lemon

Sea salt and freshly ground black pepper

Romaine lettuce leaves for serving

Soak the farro in water to cover for at least 1 hour
or overnight.

In a large, heavy saucepan, heat the 3 tablespoons
olive oil over medium-high heat. Add the green
onions, garlic, zucchini, and bell pepper and sauté
until softened, about 2 minutes. Add the stock and
bring to a boil. Drain the farro and add to the pan,
cover, and decrease the heat to a simmer. Cook for
30 to 40 minutes, or until the farro is tender and
the stock has been absorbed. Stir in the chickpeas
and salame. Cover and set aside to keep warm.

In a small bowl, whisk the lemon zest, lemon juice,
and the remaining ¹/₄ cup olive oil together. Season
with salt and pepper to taste.

Fluff the farro with a fork. Stir in the dressing. Serve
warm or chilled, on lettuce leaves.

SERVES 6

Panzanella

Bread Salad

Panzanella is one of several classic recipes using dry or day-old bread. Many American versions use croutons, but the authentic version is made with a dry bread that is soaked in water to reconstitute it, then is mixed with tomato, cucumber, basil, and onion, and dressed with olive oil and vinegar. In hard times, it was often made with just bread and onion, but today you may see such additions as tuna, green beans, bell peppers, anchovies, hard-boiled eggs, and capers.

1 pound day-old country-style bread, cut into several pieces

2 large ripe tomatoes, seeded and diced

1 cucumber, peeled, seeded, and diced

1/2 cup finely chopped red onion

3 cloves garlic, minced

1/4 cup red wine vinegar

1/3 cup extra-virgin olive oil

Sea salt and freshly ground black pepper

3 sprigs basil for garnish

Crumble the bread in a large bowl and add water to cover. Let soak for 15 minutes. Squeeze the bread with your hands and discard the soaking water. Place the bread in a medium bowl with the tomatoes, cucumber, and red onion.

In a small bowl, combine the garlic and vinegar. Gradually whisk in the olive oil. Season with salt and pepper to taste.

Toss the dressing with the bread mixture, then garnish with basil sprigs and serve at once.

SERVES 6

Polenta di Castagna con Salsicce

CHESTNUT POLENTA WITH FRESH SAUSAGE

This dish was daily fare for mountain people during hard times, served plain, or sometimes with ricotta or onions. On special occasions, it was served with sausages or cheese, a delectable foil for the sweetness of the chestnut flour. A copper pot works very well for cooking this dish, which is made just like corn polenta.

4 cups water

2 tablespoons extra-virgin olive oil, plus more for brushing

1 teaspoon sea salt

1 teaspoon minced fresh rosemary

2 1/2 cups chestnut flour, sifted

1 pound Italian-style pork sausages, butterflied

In a large, heavy pot, bring the water to a boil over high heat, and add the 2 tablespoons olive oil, the salt, and rosemary. Decrease the heat to medium and gradually whisk in the chestnut flour in a fine stream. Continue to cook for 15 to 20 minutes, stirring frequently, until the polenta pulls away from the side of the pan.

Meanwhile, light a medium-hot fire in a charcoal grill. Lightly brush the sausages with oil and grill them until nicely browned, about 5 minutes on each side. Transfer to a plate.

Serve immediately, with the sausages arranged on top.

VARIATION: Turn the polenta into an oiled jelly roll pan and let cool until firm, about 20 minutes. Cut into squares to serve or grill.

SERVES 4

Polenta di Mais di Otto File

CORN POLENTA

My friend Andrea Bertucci has an osteria called
Il Vecchio Mulino in the Tuscan mountain village of
Castelnuovo Garfagnana. Here, you can taste local
varieties of beans and grains in traditional preparations,
such as this polenta made from an antique kind of corn
called formenton otto file (the otto file refers to the
eight rows of kernels on each ear). Andrea introduced
me to Giordano Andreucci, chef/owner of Ristorante Il
Pozzo in Castelnuovo Garfagnana, who shared his
mother's recipe for making the polenta, a layered dish
with ragù and cheese. Giordano says this dish is best
made with freshly ground polenta, and explains that
the roscata, the part where kernel attaches to ear, is
smaller in formenton and grinds better. If you are
unable to find a coarse stone-ground cornmeal,
substitute a finer meal, but decrease the cooking time
by half. The polenta is finished when it is thick and
pulls away from the sides of the pot.

4 cups spring water

1 tablespoon extra-virgin olive oil

Pinch of salt

3 cups coarsely ground cornmeal, preferably otto
    file (see Resources), or polenta

4 cups Ragù (page 88)

1 cup grated pecorino cheese

Lightly oil an 8-inch-square baking dish.

In a large, heavy saucepan, combine the water, oil,
and salt, and bring to a boil over high heat. Gradually
whisk in the polenta in a fine stream. Decrease the
heat to medium and cook, stirring constantly, for
30 to 40 minutes, or until the polenta thickens and
comes away from the sides of the pot.

Spoon about 1 cup polenta into the prepared baking
dish and smooth the top. Cover with a layer of about
1/2 cup of ragù, then repeat until the dish is filled,
ending with a layer of ragù. Sprinkle with the cheese.
Cover with a damp dish towel and let stand for 15 to
20 minutes before serving. Cut into squares to serve.

SERVES 4

Pici all'Aglione
PASTA WITH GARLIC-TOMATO SAUCE

*Pici is a hand-rolled fresh pasta from the southern part
of the province of Siena. Each strand is rolled by hand.
The classic sauce is aglione, made with wild garlic and
tomatoes. If your farmers' market sells green garlic, you
will come close to the traditional recipe. Otherwise, just
substitute regular garlic. My friend Lina Mazzetti's
secret? Warm water in the dough.*

AGLIONE SAUCE

6 very ripe tomatoes, peeled, seeded, and coarsely
    chopped

1 small head green garlic, or 3 regular garlic
    cloves, sliced

2 tablespoons extra-virgin olive oil

2 dried *peperoncini* (dried red peppers), or
    red pepper flakes to taste

1/4 cup minced fresh flat-leaf parsley

Sea salt and freshly ground black pepper

PICI DOUGH

4 cups unbleached all-purpose flour

1 1/4 cups warm water

1 tablespoon extra-virgin olive oil, plus
    1 teaspoon for rubbing on the dough

Pinch of salt

Coarse semolina flour or cornmeal

For the sauce: In a large saucepan, combine the
tomatoes, garlic, olive oil, *peperoncini*, and parsley.
Bring to a simmer over medium heat and cook for
30 to 35 minutes, stirring occasionally, until the garlic
is very tender. Season with salt and pepper to taste.
Pass through a food mill or purée with an immersion
blender. Set aside and keep warm, or reheat to serve.

Meanwhile, for the *pici* dough: Mound the flour on
a wooden board and make a well in the center. Add
the water, 1 tablespoon of the olive oil, and salt to the
well. With your hands (or a fork), work the flour into
the liquid from the sides to make a smooth dough.
Clean the board, lightly flour it, then knead the dough
for about 15 minutes, or until smooth and elastic.
Lightly rub with the remaining 1 teaspoon olive oil,
then cover with a damp towel or plastic wrap and let
rest for 20 to 30 minutes.

Flatten the dough and cut into thin strips. Roll, one
at a time, on the board with the palms of your hands
into a long, round strand, like a fat spaghetti. Lay
the strands out on a tray liberally sprinkled with
semolina or cornmeal to keep them from sticking.

Cook in a large pot of salted boiling water, cook the
pici for 3 to 4 minutes, until al dente. Drain and toss
with the sauce. Serve at once.

SERVES 4

Tagliatelle al Ragù di Domenica
TAGLIATELLE WITH SUNDAY MEAT SAUCE

The big batch of meat sauce made for the Sunday pasta could also be used in Baked Pasta (page 89) and on polenta. It is likely that in harder times, there were more tomatoes and liquid and just one kind of chopped or ground meat. The meat can be veal or beef, wild boar, pork, rabbit, duck, or game; just adjust the cooking time to be sure the meat is very tender. The longer the sauce simmers, the better the flavors marry.

RAGÙ

1/4 cup extra-virgin olive oil

1 onion, finely chopped

1 stalk celery, finely chopped

1 carrot, finely chopped

8 ounces Italian-style pork sausages,
   casings removed

8 ounces finely ground pork

1/2 cup dry red wine

1 cup meat stock (page 172)

1 (14 1/2-ounce) can peeled whole tomatoes
   with juice, coarsely chopped

A few gratings of nutmeg

Sea salt and freshly ground black pepper

24 ounces tagliatelle pasta

For the ragù: In a large saucepan, heat the olive oil over medium-high heat. Add the onion, celery, and carrot and cook for 5 to 6 minutes, or until golden brown.

Crumble in the sausage meat and ground meat and cook until browned. Add the wine and stir to scrape up the browned bits from the bottom of the pan. Increase the heat to high and cook until the liquid is reduced by half. Add the stock and tomatoes. Decrease the heat to a simmer and cook, stirring frequently, for 35 to 40 minutes, or until thickened. The longer you cook this, the better it tastes; if you do cook it longer, keep adding broth to keep the sauce from scorching. Season to taste with nutmeg, salt, and pepper.

In a large pot of salted boiling water, cook the pasta according to package directions until al dente. Drain and toss with sauce, reserving 1/2 cup to spoon on top. Turn into warmed serving bowl, spoon the reserved sauce on top, and serve at once.

MAKES ABOUT 8 CUPS RAGÙ; SERVES 8 TO 10

Pasta al Forno

Baked Pasta

This dish has long been a way to use up leftover sauce and maltagliati *(bits of leftover fresh pasta, literally "badly cut"). Freshly boiled or leftover shaped pasta, such as penne, works equally well. The balsamella (béchamel) sauce is the same binding element used to make the more elaborate pasta al forno known as lasagna, made with sheets of fresh pasta.*

8 ounces shaped pasta, such as penne
    or rigatoni

BALSAMELLA

4 cups milk

6 tablespoons extra-virgin olive oil,
    plus more for tossing

$^1/_4$ cup unbleached all-purpose flour

$^1/_2$ teaspoon sea salt and freshly ground
    black pepper

Freshly grated nutmeg

4 cups Ragù (page 88)

$^1/_2$ cup grated Parmigiano-Reggiano cheese

1 bunch basil, stemmed and julienned

Preheat the oven to 350°F. Lightly oil a 9 by 13-inch baking dish.

In a large pot of salted boiling water, cook the pasta according to the package directions until al dente. Drain, toss with olive oil, and set aside.

For the *balsamella*: In a large saucepan, heat the milk over medium heat until bubbles form around the edges of the pan. In another saucepan, warm the olive oil over medium heat. Whisk in the flour and cook for 1 to 2 minutes, or until foamy. Gradually whisk in the hot milk and return to medium heat. Cook, whisking constantly, for 3 to 4 minutes, or until thickened. Season with salt, pepper, and nutmeg to taste. Remove about 1 cup of the *balsamella* and set aside in a warm place. Add the ragù and cooked pasta to the remaining *balsamella* in the saucepan. Mix well.

Spread half of the reserved *balsamella* evenly in the bottom of the prepared baking dish. Transfer the meat mixture to the baking dish and smooth the top. Cover the top with the remaining reserved *balsamella*, smooth the top, and sprinkle evenly with the cheese. Bake for 30 to 40 minutes, or until lightly browned. Sprinkle with julienned basil and serve at once.

SERVES 8

Gnudi

SPINACH AND RICOTTA DUMPLINGS

Gnudi *means, well, "nude"—because these are nude ravioli, the filling without the outer pasta covering. They are delicious served with tomato sauce, as in this recipe, or with melted butter and sage.*

3/4 cup steamed spinach (see page 175), finely chopped

3/4 cup whole-milk ricotta cheese

1/2 cup grated pecorino or Parmigiano-Reggiano cheese

2 large egg yolks

1/4 teaspoon freshly grated nutmeg

1/2 teaspoon sea salt

1 cup unbleached all-purpose flour

3 cups tomato sauce (page 173)

In a large bowl, combine the spinach, ricotta, pecorino, and egg yolks. Stir to blend. Stir in the nutmeg and salt to taste, then gently stir in the flour, mixing just enough to pull the mixture together.

Bring a large pot of salted water to a boil. Heat the tomato sauce and spread a thin layer of it over the bottom of a 9 by 13-inch baking dish. Set aside.

Using two tablespoons, shape and compact the ricotta mixture into ovals and drop them directly into the boiling water in batches, so as not to crowd the pot. They will float to the top when done, after 3 to 4 minutes. Using a wire skimmer or slotted spoon, transfer the *gnudi* to the casserole dish. Keep warm in a low oven. Repeat to cook all the remaining *gnudi*. Spoon the remaining tomato sauce over the *gnudi* and serve at once.

SERVES 6

Pasta alle Briciole
PASTA WITH SPICY BREAD CRUMB TOPPING

The topping for this pasta is sometimes called poor man's Parmigiano and represents cucina povera at its most frugal. Women would save every bread crumb until there were enough to dress pasta, garnish soups, or flavor roasted or grilled vegetables. For this recipe, the breadcrumbs are tossed with garlic and spicy red pepper flakes that have been sautéed in olive oil. The finished topping is crunchy with a wonderful, spicy flavor.

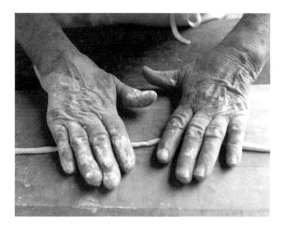

1 pound pasta (such as *pici*, [page 87], *bucatini*, or spaghetti)

3 cups coarse dried bread crumbs

3 cloves garlic, minced

Pinch of red pepper flakes

1/4 cup extra-virgin olive oil

In a large pot of salted boiling water, cook the pasta according to the package directions until al dente.

Meanwhile, heat the oil in a large skillet over medium heat and sauté the bread, garlic, and pepper flakes until the crumbs are golden. Using a slotted spoon, transfer to paper towels to drain and let cool.

Drain the pasta, add the topping, and toss. Serve at once.

SERVES 6

Penne al Sugo di Lepre
PASTA WITH WILD HARE OR RABBIT SAUCE

This hearty recipe comes from the Lunigiana, the mountainous region of Tuscany touching Liguria on the northwest. In Italy, all parts of a hare or rabbit are used, including the organs and lungs. Domestic rabbit can be substituted, if you like; ask your butcher to cut it up for you, and to include the heart and liver. Many recipes also call for tomatoes, but I like the meatiness of the sauce without it. Both rabbit and hare are very lean, so be sure the meat is always bathed in liquid, and let it cook slowly.

1 young hare or rabbit, about 3 pounds, including heart and liver

2 cups dry red wine

1 cup extra-virgin olive oil, plus 3 tablespoons for tossing

1 clove garlic, minced

1 teaspoon minced fresh thyme

1 bay leaf

4 or 5 whole peppercorns

1 carrot, peeled and finely chopped

1 stalk celery, finely chopped

1 onion, finely chopped

Flour for dredging

4 cups chicken stock (page 173), heated

1 teaspoon dried juniper berries

2 whole cloves

1/2 cup Italian oil-cured black olives, pitted

Sea salt and freshly ground black pepper

1 pound penne pasta

1/2 cup pine nuts, toasted (see page 175)

Cut the hare into 8 pieces. Rinse the hare, heart, and liver and let drain.

In a large nonreactive container, combine the wine, $^1/_2$ cup of the olive oil, the garlic, thyme, bay leaf, and peppercorns. Add the hare and the heart and liver, cover, and refrigerate for at least 2 hours or overnight.

Remove the hare from the refrigerator 30 minutes before cooking and drain it, reserving the marinade and the heart and liver. In a large sauté pan, heat the remaining $^1/_2$ cup olive oil over medium heat. Add the carrot, celery, and onion and sauté for 5 to 6 minutes, or until the onion is golden brown. Dredge the pieces of hare in the flour; add to the pan and brown for about 4 minutes on each side. Add the reserved marinade to the pan and stir to scrape up the browned bits from the bottom of the pan. Increase the heat to medium-high and cook to reduce the marinade by half. Add the stock, juniper berries, and cloves and bring to a simmer.

Coarsely chop the heart and liver and add to the pan. Decrease the heat to low, cover, and cook for another $1^1/_2$ hours, or until the meat is tender and falling off the bone. Remove the pieces of hare and debone, then return the meat to the pan to reheat with the black olives. Season with salt and pepper to taste.

In a large pot of salted boiling water, cook the pasta according to package directions until al dente. Drain and toss with olive oil. Turn into a warmed serving bowl and spoon the sauce on top. Sprinkle with the pine nuts and serve at once.

Serves 6

Tortelli di Patate del Mugello con Burro Fuso e Salvia

TORTELLI WITH POTATO FILLING AND MELTED BUTTER AND SAGE

This rich and comforting dish comes from the Mugello, in the hills above Florence. It is a special-occasion dish, served on August 10 for the feast of San Lorenzo.

1/4 cup extra-virgin olive oil

1 carrot, peeled and finely chopped

1 stalk celery, finely chopped

1/2 onion, finely chopped

1/2 cup dry white wine

1 pound boiling potatoes, cooked, peeled, and diced (about 2 cups)

1/4 cup freshly grated pecorino or Parmigiano-Reggiano cheese, plus 1/4 cup more for serving

3 large eggs, beaten

1/2 teaspoon sea salt

Freshly ground black pepper

1 pound fresh pasta dough (page 174), rolled into sheets

1/2 cup (1 stick) unsalted butter

24 small fresh sage leaves

In a medium sauté pan, heat the olive oil over medium-high heat and sauté the carrot, celery, and onion until golden brown, 5 to 6 minutes. Add the wine and stir to scrape up the browned bits from the bottom of the pan. Stir in the potatoes, increase the heat to high, and cook for 3 to 4 minutes, or until thickened. Pass the mixture through a ricer or a food mill. Set aside and let cool completely. Fold in 1/4 cup cheese and the eggs. Season to taste with salt and pepper.

In a small bowl, beat the remaining egg with a fork. Place a sheet of pasta on a lightly floured work surface. Place teaspoonfuls of filling at regular intervals about 3 inches apart, with a 3-inch border all around the pasta sheet. Lightly brush the exposed pasta with the beaten egg. Top with a second sheet of pasta, and press with your fingers along the edges and around each mound of filling to seal. Cut out the tortelli with a biscuit cutter or pastry wheel. Set aside on a lightly floured dish towel until ready to cook.

In a saucepan, melt the butter. Add the sage leaves and simmer for 5 minutes. Remove from the heat and keep warm.

In a large pot of salted boiling water, cook the pasta for about 2 minutes, or until al dente. Drain and toss with the butter and sage. Transfer to a warmed platter, sprinkle with the remaining cheese, and serve at once.

SERVES 6

Chi ha vitella in tavola
non mangia cipolla.

Those who have veal at the table don't have to eat onions.

Meats & Seafood

STINCO DI MAIALE 100
Braised Pork Shanks

INVOLTINI DI MAIALE 103
Pork Rolls Stuffed with Ricotta and Spinach

CINGHIALE E CARCIOFI IN UMIDO 104
Wild Boar and Artichokes

FEGATELLI ALLA FIORENTINA 105
Florentine Pork Livers

CONIGLIO CON I FUNGHI 106
Rabbit and Mushrooms

TRIPPA ALLA FIORENTINA 109
Florentine Tripe

POLPETTONE 110
Meat Loaf

PICCIONE FARCITO ALLO SPIEDO 111
Skewered Stuffed Squab

POLLO ARROSTO AL VIN SANTO 112
Roasted Chicken with Vin Santo Sauce

PEPOSO DI GUANCIALE 115
Stewed Peppery Beef Cheeks

BRASATO AL MIDOLLO 116
Braised Beef with Marrow and Shallots

TOTANI RIPIENI 120
Stuffed Squid

TEGAMACCIO DI PESCE 122
Freshwater Fish Stew

POLPO ALL'ELBANA 123
Octopus from Elba Island

BACCALÀ IN ZIMINO 124
Salted Cod with Greens

TRIGLIE ALLA LIVORNESE 125
Mullet with Garlic, Parsley, and Tomatoes

BRUSTICO 126
Grilled Freshwater Fish

Stinco di Maiale

BRAISED PORK SHANKS

Most cooks are familiar with osso buco, a dish made with veal or beef shanks. In Tuscany, a land where the pig is king, a simplified version of osso buco is made with pork and given a different name. This recipe uses the classic technique of slow-cooking a lean, inexpensive cut of meat in liquid until tender.

2 pork shanks, about 1 pound each, cut into 2-inch-thick crosswise slices

4 medium carrots, peeled and cut into 1/2-inch-thick rounds

2 large onions, coarsely chopped

4 medium potatoes, peeled and cubed

Sea salt and freshly ground black pepper

Rinse the shanks and put them in a heavy pot with cold water to cover. Bring the liquid to a low boil, decrease the heat to a simmer, cover, and cook for 1 1/2 hours. Add the carrots, onions, potatoes, and salt and pepper to taste. Cover and cook for 45 minutes, or until the meat and vegetables are fork-tender. Transfer to a warmed platter and serve.

SERVES 4

Involtini di Maiale

PORK ROLLS STUFFED WITH RICOTTA AND SPINACH

In the modern kitchen, these cutlets are made with veal or chicken breasts, but pork is absolutely divine and more economical. In this past, this dish would have been made with thin slices of boneless pork shoulder, and the rolls would have been braised in plenty of liquid to tenderize it. Wrapping the meat with pancetta helps keep it moist.

8 ounces spinach, steamed (see page 175) and finely chopped

$^1/_2$ cup whole-milk ricotta cheese

Sea salt and freshly ground black pepper

Freshly grated nutmeg

1 pound boneless pork loin, sliced into 8 pieces

8 thin slices pancetta

$^1/_4$ cup extra-virgin olive oil

1 cup dry white wine

In a medium bowl, combine the spinach and ricotta and stir to blend. Season with salt, pepper, and nutmeg to taste. Set aside.

Place a slice of pork between 2 pieces of parchment paper, and roll with a rolling pin until flattened to an even thickness, about $^1/_8$ inch. Repeat to flatten the remaining slices.

Spread a thin layer of the spinach mixture on top of a slice of pork, leaving a $^1/_4$-inch border. Roll it and wrap with a slice of pancetta, then fasten with a toothpick. Repeat with the remaining pork, filling, and pancetta.

In a large, heavy sauté pan, heat the olive oil over medium-high heat, and sear the rolls for about 2 minutes on each side. Add the wine and stir to scrape up the browned bits from the bottom of the pan. Simmer briskly for 7 to 8 minutes, turning the rolls once or twice to heat them through. Serve at once.

SERVES 4

Cinghiale e Carciofi in Umido
WILD BOAR AND ARTICHOKES

The hunting season for wild boar begins on the first weekend in November, but we won't be eating fresh boar for another week, as it needs to age for several days before cooking. During the rest of the year, frozen boar is available; the freezing process actually helps to tenderize the meat. In any case, this lean meat needs to be braised to make it truly tender.

1/2 cup extra-virgin olive oil

1 onion, finely chopped

2 carrots, peeled and finely chopped

1 stalk celery, finely chopped

4 pounds wild boar (*cinghiale*), cut into
    serving-size pieces

3 tablespoons minced garlic

1 (750-ml) bottle dry red wine

1/4 cup minced fresh rosemary

2 tablespoons dried juniper berries

2 to 2 1/2 cups meat stock (page 172), heated

8 large artichokes, trimmed into hearts
    and cut into eighths (page 175)

2 large fennel bulbs, cored and thinly sliced

Sea salt and freshly ground black pepper

In a Dutch oven or heatproof casserole, heat 1/4 cup of the olive oil over medium heat and sauté the onion, carrots, and celery for 4 to 5 muinutes, or until the onion is golden. Add the boar and sauté until browned on all sides, about 2 minutes on each side.

Add the garlic and wine and stir to scrape up the browned bits from the bottom of the pan. Cook to reduce the liquid by half, then decrease the heat to a simmer. Add the stock, rosemary, and juniper berries, cover, and cook for about 2 hours, or until the meat is tender, adding additional stock if needed to keep the meat moist.

In a large, heavy skillet, heat the remaining 1/4 cup olive oil in a large skillet and add the artichokes. Sauté for 7 to 8 minutes, or until softened. Add the fennel and sauté for 2 to 3 minutes, or until softened. Add the vegetable mixture to the pot with the meat. Season with salt and pepper to taste and serve.

SERVES 8

Fegatelli alla Fiorentina

FLORENTINE PORK LIVERS

This dish was a winter delicacy in medieval times, when pork livers were available at the time of the annual slaughtering of pigs. Today, these little morsels are found in Tuscan butcher shops year round, ready for roasting or grilling. Here is how to make them yourself, though you will probably need to ask your butcher to order the caul fat, the lacy membrane that will hold the liver in shape and keep it moist.

1 pound pork livers

6 ounces caul fat

1/3 cup minced fresh flat-leaf parsley

2 tablespoons minced fresh marjoram

1 teaspoon fennel flowers or seeds

Pinch of ground cloves

2 tablespoons dried bread crumbs

Sea salt and freshly ground black pepper

3 tablespoons extra-virgin olive oil

1 cup dry red wine

1 bay leaf

Preheat the oven to 375°F. Lightly oil an 8-inch-square baking dish.

Cut the pork livers into 2-inch cubes and set aside. Rinse the caul fat and cut it into 6-inch-square pieces. Set aside in cold water.

In a small bowl, combine the parsley, marjoram, fennel flowers, cloves, and bread crumbs. Season with salt and pepper to taste and set aside.

In a large, heavy sauté pan, heat the olive oil over medium heat. Add the liver cubes and sear quickly on all sides, 2 to 3 minutes. Remove from the heat and toss with the herb mixture to coat evenly. Wrap each piece of liver in a square of caul fat and secure it with a toothpick. Place the wrapped liver cubes in the prepared baking dish. Add the wine and bay leaf to the remaining herb mixture and pour over the livers.

Bake for 12 to 15 minutes, or until the caul has rendered its fat and dissolves. Remove the bay leaf and serve.

SERVES 6

Coniglio con i Funghi

RABBIT AND MUSHROOMS

Rabbits, as we know, multiply quickly, and for this reason they were a staple in the peasant farm kitchen. This lean meat needs braising, or as here, it may be roasted as long as some fatty ingredient such as pancetta is added to keep it moist. This is lovely served over polenta (page 85).

1 rabbit, about 2 pounds, cut into serving pieces

3 cups dry white wine

1 sprig rosemary

2 cloves garlic

5 dried juniper berries

1/4 cup extra-virgin olive oil

1 pound mushrooms, sliced

2 cups chicken stock (page 173), heated

Sea salt and freshly ground black pepper

Place the rabbit in a nonreactive container and add the wine, rosemary, garlic, and juniper berries. Let stand at room temperature for at least 30 minutes or up to 1 hour, or 2 hours to overnight in the refrigerator. Transfer the rabbit to a sieve set over a bowl and drain, reserving the marinade.

In a large, heavy sauté pan, heat the olive oil, and brown the rabbit for about 2 minutes on each side. Add the mushrooms and sauté until softened, 3 to 4 minutes. Add the strained marinade and stir to scrape up the browned bits from the bottom of the pan. Add the chicken stock, cover, and cook for 20 to 30 minutes, or until the rabbit is tender. Season with salt and pepper to taste.

SERVES 4

Trippa alla Fiorentina
FLORENTINE TRIPE

Today trippa and lampredotto are popular Florentine street food and a delicacy at home, though in the past they were considered food for the poor. Tripe is the inner lining of the first of a cow's four stomachs, while lampredotto comes from the fourth stomach. The tripe most commonly found in the States, which resembles a honeycomb and comes from the second stomach, can be used in this recipe.

Miriam Serni Casalini (page 33) has written much about Tuscan kitchen wisdom in her book Il Buglione, and trippa is one of her specialties. Nowadays she adds a tablespoon of butter and a sprinkle of grated Parmigiano-Reggiano cheese to richen the dish. Trippa is also delicious as a sandwich with salsa verde (a green sauce made with parsley, capers, garlic, and anchovies).

1 pound tripe, cut into thin strips

$^1/_4$ cup extra-virgin olive oil

1 onion, diced

1 pound tomatoes, peeled, seeded, and coarsely chopped (page 175)

Sea salt and freshly ground black pepper

Place the tripe in a medium saucepan, cover, and cook over low heat until it has dried, about 15 minutes. Rinse at once in cold water and let drain.

In a heavy, medium saucepan, heat the olive oil over medium-high heat, and cook the onion until softened, 3 to 4 minutes. Add the tomatoes and tripe, and decrease the heat to low. Cover and cook for 30 minutes, or until the tripe is tender. Season with salt and pepper to taste.

SERVES 4

Polpettone
Meat Loaf

My friend Lina Mazzetti often makes this meat loaf with a carrot in the center so that cut slices have a piece of the vegetable. The carrot should be peeled, then boiled in salted water for about 5 minutes and cooled before shaping the meat around it.

1/2 cup extra-virgin olive oil

1/2 cup finely chopped onion

1/3 cup finely chopped carrot

1/3 cup finely chopped celery

1 1/2 pounds mixed lean ground meats
(beef, veal, and/or pork)

3 fresh Italian-style pork sausages
(about 8 ounces), casings removed

2 large eggs, beaten

1/2 cup fine dried bread crumbs

3 tablespoons minced fresh flat-leaf parsley

2 teaspoons sea salt, plus more for seasoning

Flour for dredging

1 cup dry red wine

2 cups meat stock (page 172), heated

4 boiling potatoes, peeled and diced

Freshly ground black pepper

Preheat the oven to 375°F. In a medium skillet, heat 1/4 cup of the olive oil over medium heat, and sauté the onion, carrot, and celery for 5 to 6 minutes, or until the onion is golden brown. Set aside to cool.

In a large bowl, combine the ground meats, sausage meat, eggs, bread crumbs, 2 tablespoons of the parsley, and the 2 teaspoons salt. Add the sautéed vegetables and mix well. Shape it into an oblong loaf, compact well, and gently dredge it in flour.

In a Dutch oven or large ovenproof casserole, heat the remaining 1/4 cup olive oil. Carefully transfer the meat roll to the pan and brown on all sides, turning gently, about 2 minutes on each side. Add the wine to the pan, stir to scrape up the browned bits from the bottom of the pan, and cook to reduce the liquid slightly. Add the stock, the potatoes, and the remaining 1 tablespoon parsley to the liquid in the pan. Cover and bake for 25 to 30 minutes. Season the sauce with salt and pepper to taste. Let rest for 10 minutes before slicing. Cut into slices and serve with the sauce spooned over.

Serves 6 to 8

Piccione Farcito allo Spiedo
SKEWERED STUFFED SQUAB

Other small birds can be used for this recipe, such as quail or Cornish hens or even chicken, but the cooking time will need to be adjusted. When done, an instant-read thermometer inserted in the thigh and not touching bone will register 165°F, or the juices will run clear when the thigh is pierced with a knife. If you don't have a rotisserie, simply use metal skewers and turn the birds on the grill every 10 minutes.

6 squabs

Extra-virgin olive oil for coating, plus oil for basting

Sea salt for sprinkling

3 slices country-style bread (3 ounces), crusts removed

1/2 cup whole milk

4 Italian-style pork sausages

5 ounces pancetta, diced

3 tablespoons raisins

3 tablespoons pine nuts, toasted (page 175)

2 large egg yolks, beaten

A few gratings of nutmeg

Sea salt and freshly ground black pepper

2 onions, cut into wedges

Prepare a medium-hot indirect fire in a charcoal grill fitted with a rotisserie. Coat the squabs with olive oil and sprinkle with salt. Set aside.

Tear the bread into pieces and place in a medium bowl. Add the milk and let stand for 10 minutes, or until softened. Remove the casings from half of the sausages. Add the sausage meat, pancetta, raisins, and pine nuts to the bowl with the bread and milk. Add the egg yolks and mix well. Season with nutmeg, salt, and pepper to taste. Stuff one-sixth of the meat mixture into the body cavity of each squab. Close the openings with toothpicks.

Cut the remaining sausages into 2-inch lengths. Skewer the squabs crosswise, inserting the spit just under the wings and alternating each bird with a piece of sausage and a wedge of onion. Grill the pigeons over the indirect fire for about 30 minutes, or until they test done, basting them periodically with olive oil, if needed.

SERVES 6

Pollo Arrosto al Vin Santo
ROASTED CHICKEN WITH VIN SANTO SAUCE

Vin santo is a Tuscan dessert wine made with dried grapes. Marsala makes a good substitute, or you can use a good dry white wine. Adjust the cooking time according to the size of chicken you use. When the chicken is done, an instant-read thermometer inserted in a thigh and not touching bone will register 165°F, or the juices will run clear when a thigh is pierced with a knife.

3 tablespoons aromatic herbs minced with salt (page 41), or your preferred combination of fresh herbs

1 clove garlic, minced

1 chicken, about 3 pounds

3 tablespoons extra-virgin olive oil

Sea salt and freshly ground black pepper

2 cups vin santo or sweet Marsala wine

Preheat the oven to 400°F. Lightly oil a small roasting pan or heatproof casserole.

In a small bowl, combine the herb mixture with the garlic. Loosen the skin of the breast of the chicken and spread the herb mixture under the skin. Rub the chicken all over with the olive oil and season with salt and pepper. Place the chicken on its side in the prepared pan and roast for 15 minutes, then turn and roast on the second side for 15 minutes. Turn the chicken onto its back and roast for 30 minutes, or until the chicken tests done.

Transfer the chicken to a serving platter and keep warm. Set the roasting pan over medium heat and add the wine, stirring to scrape up the browned bits from the bottom of the pan. Increase the heat to high and cook to reduce the liquid by half. Drizzle the pan sauce over the roasted chicken and serve at once.

SERVES 6

Peposo di Guanciale

STEWED PEPPERY BEEF CHEEKS

Recipes with once-exotic spices such as peppercorns, cinnamon, and cloves are traditionally Florentine or Sienese, as those cities were involved in the Renaissance spice trade. Food writer Kyle Phillips dates peposo back to the time when Florence's Duomo was being built and the tile makers would stew tough cuts of meat in their kilns. Often made with beef shank or other lean stewing meat, I love this version made with beef cheeks.

1/2 cup extra-virgin olive oil

1 carrot, peeled and finely chopped

1 stalk celery, finely chopped

1 small onion, finely chopped

2 pounds beef cheeks, cubed

1 (750-ml) bottle dry red wine

3 tablespoons black peppercorns

2 bay leaves

Sea salt

Preheat the oven to 375°F. In a Dutch oven or large heatproof casserole, heat the olive oil over medium heat. Add the carrot, celery, and onion and sauté for 5 to 6 minutes, or until the onion is golden brown. Add the beef and cook until browned on all sides. Add the wine and stir to scrape up the browned bits from the bottom of the pan. Add the peppercorns and bay leaves.

Cover and bake for at least 20 minutes, then decrease the heat to 275°F and cook for at least 1 hour, or until very tender. Season to taste with salt. Remove the bay leaves and serve.

SERVES 6 TO 8

Brasato al Midollo
BRAISED BEEF WITH MARROW AND SHALLOTS

Dario Cecchini, the legendary butcher of Panzano in Chianti, offered me this recipe, which, he explained, is *povera* only in the sense that the shank is an inexpensive cut of meat. Long, slow cooking transforms it into a superbly flavorful dish. Ask your butcher to butterfly the meat, remove the bone, and saw it in half lengthwise to make the marrow easier to remove. Save the bone halves in the freezer for making stock.

1 whole beef shank (about 8 pounds), boned and butterflied, bone sawed in half lengthwise and reserved

2 tablespoons sea salt

2 tablespoons freshly ground black pepper

Leaves from 3 sprigs rosemary, plus 3 whole sprigs

1¹⁄2 pounds medium shallots

¹⁄4 cup olive oil

1¹⁄2 cups vin santo or dry white wine

(recipe continued on page 118)

TUSCAN BUTCHER

The colorful and charismatic Dario Cecchini is known to Italians and foreigners alike as the "poet butcher of Panzano in Chianti." He is renowned for his dramatic interpretations of Dante and his favorite songs, but most of all for his passion for his profession. Above all, Dario is interested in respecting the 250-year Cecchini family tradition of the art of meat cutting, evident in his choice of quality meat and products for his butcher shop, the joyful Antica Macelleria.

"Everyone comes into the shop to buy the prime cuts," he said to me a few years ago. "The loin, the steak, the rump of the cow, the pig, or the lamb are in high demand. What about the rest of the animal?" This was the question that inspired his restaurant, Solociccia ("Only Meat"), a place where the "rest of the animal" finds a privileged place at the table. Rather than taking meat for granted, he elevates all parts of it in traditional ways. Here you will find beef shins filled with their own marrow and braised for hours; tenerumi (beef knee) with a salad of fresh vegetables; and chopped meats coaxed into savory meatballs speared with rosemary. These and all the other offerings at Dario's restaurant exalt humble ingredients in the best traditions of Tuscan cuisine. In Dario's words, "In a correct world, we should try to use everything wisely. When someone wastes, someone else suffers."

Brasato al Midollo *(continued)*

Preheat the oven to 375°F. Season the meat on both sides with salt and pepper. Place the meat on a cutting board, cut side up. Scoop the marrow from the reserved bone halves and distribute it on one half of the meat. Sprinkle the rosemary leaves over the marrow. Roll the meat into a log, and tie tightly in at least 4 places with kitchen string.

Place the meat in a Dutch oven or other heavy pot with a lid. Add the rosemary sprigs and scatter the shallots over and around the meat. Drizzle the olive oil over the meat and shallots. Cover and roast for 1½ hours. Uncover and pour the wine over the meat. Using tongs, turn the meat over in the pot and replace the lid. Roast for another hour.

Remove the pot from the oven and turn the meat over again. Baste with the pan juices and return to

the oven, uncovered. Roast for 30 minutes, or until the meat is tender and browned. Remove from the oven, transfer the meat to a cutting board, and cover loosely with aluminum foil. Let rest for 15 minutes.

Using a slotted spoon, transfer the shallots to a warmed serving platter. Pour the pan juices into a gravy separator or pitcher and let the fat rise to the top. Pour or spoon off the fat, reserving the pan juices.

Remove the strings from the meat and cut the meat into 1/2-inch-thick slices. Arrange the slices on the serving platter with the shallots, and pour some of the pan juices over all. Serve with the remaining pan juices on the side.

SERVES 6 TO 8

Totani Ripieni
STUFFED SQUID

Totani are members of the squid family that resemble common squid, or calamari, and are interchangeable with them in recipes. The small ones are very tender and quick to prepare. You can buy squid already cleaned, or clean them yourself (see the note at the end of the recipe). Here, they are stuffed with a simple filling that can be enhanced with minced clams or mussels and capers. These are delicious served over pasta.

1 pound small *totani* or calamari, cleaned (see note), tentacles reserved

6 slices dry or day-old country-style bread, soaked in water and squeezed

1/4 cup minced fresh flat-leaf parsley

1 large egg, beaten

3 cloves garlic, minced

Sea salt and freshly ground black pepper

1/4 cup extra-virgin olive oil

1 small onion, sliced

2 cups tomato puree

Rinse the *totani* and pat dry.

In a medium bowl, combine the bread, parsley, egg, and garlic. Season with salt and pepper to taste. Stuff the mixture into the tubes of the *totani* and close them with a toothpick.

In a large sauté pan, heat the olive oil over medium-high heat. Add the onion and cook for 2 to 3 minutes, or until softened. Add the stuffed *totani* and sear on both sides. Add the tomato and the reserved tentacles, and decrease the heat to a simmer. Cover and cook for 1 1/2 hours, or until tender, adding water if necessary. Season with salt and pepper, and divide among shallow soup bowls. Serve at once.

SERVES 4

NOTE: To clean squid, gently twist the head (in the center of the squid) to remove it, taking care not to break the ink sac. Cut off and reserve the tentacles, removing the beak in the center. Remove the clear cartilage quill and discard. Rinse well inside and out.

Tegamaccio di Pesce

FRESHWATER FISH STEW

Tegamaccio is a term used for slow-cooked dishes (a tegame is a stew pot). It often refers to the pork stews made at hog-butchering time and incorporating the animal's blood. It may also be used for stewed eel dishes. At Lago di Chiusi, not far from my farm in Montepulciano, a type of cacciucco, or fish stew, of lake fish, is traditional. In the past, snails and frogs were also added.

2 pounds freshwater fish (such as perch, carp, eel, or pike), cleaned

$^{1}/_{2}$ cup extra-virgin olive oil

1 onion, chopped

2 cloves garlic, minced

1 *peperoncino* (dried red pepper), halved lengthwise, or pinch of red pepper flakes

1 cup dry red wine

$^{1}/_{2}$ cup red wine vinegar

8 ounces ripe tomatoes, peeled and seeded (see page 175)

1 teaspoon sea salt

1 tablespoon minced fresh thyme

If the fish are small, leave them whole; cut larger fish into pieces of equal size so the cooking time will be about the same.

In a large pot, heat the olive oil over medium-high heat, and sauté the onion for 2 to 3 minutes, or until softened. Add the garlic and *peperoncino*. Add the fish, wine, vinegar, tomatoes, salt, and thyme. Decrease the heat, cover, and cook, stirring occasionally, for 30 minutes, or until the fish is tender. Serve in warmed soup bowls.

SERVES 8

Polpo all'Elbana

OCTOPUS FROM ELBA ISLAND

*Baby octopus are popular along the coast of Tuscany,
and are found in abundance on the islands. You can
buy them cleaned or clean them yourself, reserving the
ink sac to make black risotto or pasta to serve with
the octopus. Leftovers can be made into a seafood salad
by combining with cooked potatoes and other cooked
seafood such as calamari and shrimp.*

^{1}/$_2$ cup extra-virgin olive oil

1 carrot, peeled and finely chopped

1 stalk celery, finely chopped

^{1}/$_2$ onion, finely chopped

1 ^{1}/$_2$ cups dry white wine

Juice of 1 lemon

^{1}/$_4$ cup minced fresh flat-leaf parsley

1 *peperoncino* (dried red pepper), or pinch
of red pepper flakes

3 pounds octopus, cleaned (see note) and
cut into 1-inch pieces

2 cloves garlic, minced

3 tablespoons salt-cured capers, rinsed

1 cup green olives

Sea salt and freshly ground black pepper

In a large stockpot, heat the olive oil over medium
heat, and sauté the carrot, celery, and onion for 4 to
5 minutes, or until the onion is golden. Add the wine,
lemon juice, parsley, and *peperoncino*. Bring to a boil
over high heat. Add the octopus, decrease the heat
to a simmer, cover, and cook for 1 ^{1}/$_2$ hours, or until
the octopus is easily pierced with a knife. Drain any
remaining liquid and add the garlic, capers, and olives.
Season with salt and pepper to taste, and serve at once.

SERVES 4

NOTE: To clean an octopus, rinse the octopus well.
Make a circular cut around the beak with a paring
knife, and remove the ink sac and internal organs.
Rinse the cavity well.

Baccalà in Zimino

SALTED COD WITH GREENS

Baccalà is salted codfish, widely found in the Mediterranean. In dried form, it is called stoccafisso, or stockfish. Both versions must be soaked in cold water for at least 24 hours. Baccalà needs the water frequently changed to remove the salt as it dissolves, and is sometimes left to soak under a slow stream of water. In zimino denotes fish (cod, eel, or squid) cooked with olive oil and greens, usually spinach or Swiss chard.

1 pound salted cod

3 tablespoons extra-virgin olive oil

1 small carrot, peeled and finely chopped

1 stalk celery, finely chopped

1 onion, finely chopped

Pinch of pepper flakes

1/2 cup tomato sauce (page 173)

1 pound spinach or Swiss chard, coarsely chopped

Sea salt and freshly ground black pepper

1 tablespoon minced fresh flat-leaf parsley

Soak the salt cod in cold water for 24 hours, draining and adding fresh water every 4 to 6 hours. Drain well. Cut the softened cod into 2-inch chunks and set aside.

In a large, heavy saucepan, heat the oil over medium heat, and sauté the carrot, celery, and onion for 3 to 4 minutes, or until softened. Add the pepper flakes and tomato sauce and heat for 2 to 3 minutes. Add the chard and cook for about 5 minutes, or until wilted. Decrease the heat to medium, cover, and cook for 15 minutes, or until the cod is fork-tender. Season with salt and pepper to taste, garnish with parsley, and serve at once.

SERVES 6

Triglie alla Livornese

MULLET WITH GARLIC, PARSLEY, AND TOMATOES

Red mullet is a lovely fish, but it is not widely available in the United States. Other white-fleshed fish can be substituted, such as sole, snapper, sea bass, or halibut.

3 tablespoons extra-virgin olive oil

1 pound mullet or other white-fleshed fish fillets

1 small carrot, peeled and finely chopped

1 stalk celery, finely chopped

1/2 onion, finely chopped

1 tablespoon minced fresh flat-leaf parsley

2 cloves garlic, minced

1 fresh bay leaf, or 1/2 dried bay leaf

2 tomatoes, peeled, seeded, and coarsely chopped (see page 175),

1/4 cup unbleached all-purpose flour

Sea salt and freshly ground black pepper

In a medium sauté pan, heat the oil over medium-high heat, and sauté the carrot, celery, and onion for 3 to 4 minutes, or until softened. Add the parsley, garlic, bay leaf, and tomatoes, and decrease the heat to medium.

Season the flour with salt and pepper, and dredge the fillets to coat well. Add the fillets and cook until golden, about 3 minutes on each side, turning very gently with a spatula to avoid breaking them. Remove the bay leaf and serve.

SERVES 4

Brustico

GRILLED FRESHWATER FISH

The shores of Lago di Chiusi in southern Tuscany were once the hub of an ancient Etruscan settlement. Traces of Sangiovese grapes, wheat, and olives have been found in the Etruscan tombs here, evidence of the diet of twenty-five hundred years ago. Freshwater fish from the lake were surely part of that diet as well, probably cooked over an open fire, as in this recipe.

Enrico Agostinelli at Ristorante Pesce d'Oro illustrates a time-honored method of cooking whole royal perch and pike from Lago di Chiusi over a hot fire built with the dried canes that grow at the edge of the lake. The outside of the uncleaned fish is burned black over the fast, hot fire, which cooks the delicate flesh slowly and sweetly inside. After the fish has cooled, the blackened scales are scraped off, the organs are removed, and the meat is filleted. The fillets are served at room temperature, drizzled with fresh extra-virgin olive oil, lemon, and parsley. My version, updated to be made at home, uses whole fish that have been cleaned and scaled before grilling.

6 whole perch, about 6 ounces each, cleaned

Extra-virgin olive oil for drizzling

Juice of ¹/₂ lemon, plus 1 ¹/₂ lemons, quartered

2 tablespoons minced fresh flat-leaf parsley

Prepare a hot fire in a charcoal grill using small pieces of fast-burning wood or charcoal. Place the fish on the grill, and cook for 5 to 6 minutes on each side, or until charred. Transfer to a plate and let cool slightly.

Using a knife, cut the fish in half lengthwise and remove the backbone.

Place on a serving platter and drizzle with the olive oil. Sprinkle with the lemon juice and parsley. Serve with lemon quarters.

SERVES 6

*Meglio un uovo oggi
che una gallina domani.*

Better to have an egg today than a chicken tomorrow.

Side Dishes

. . . .

FUNGHI PORCINI ALLE BRACE   130
Grilled Porcini Mushrooms with Mint and Garlic

FAGIOLI AL FIASCO   132
Baked Beans

FAGIOLI CANNELLINI   133
Cooked Cannellini Beans

ZUCCA AL FORNO   133
Baked Winter Squash

POMODORI, FAGIOLI, E CIPOLLINE   135
Roasted Tomatoes, Beans, and Onions

UOVA AI PISELLI ALLA MARELIA   136
Marelia's Peas and Eggs

CECI STUFATI   139
Stewed Chickpeas

CICORIA IN PADELLA   140
Sautéed Wild Greens

Funghi Porcini alle Brace

GRILLED PORCINI MUSHROOMS
WITH MINT AND GARLIC

After a few days of rain in the fall, then a few days of sun, the woods are filled with basket-carrying funghi hunters. The fresh Boletus edulis has a dense, meaty texture that has earned it the name "poor man's steak." This recipe can also be made with a firm mushroom such as shiitake or Portobello.

1 teaspoon minced fresh flat-leaf parsley

1 teaspoon minced fresh thyme

1 teaspoon minced fresh rosemary

1 teaspoon minced fresh mint

2 cloves garlic, minced

^{1}/$_3$ cup extra-virgin olive oil, plus more for brushing

1 pound porcini mushrooms (about 6 medium)

Light a medium fire in a charcoal grill.

In a small bowl, combine the herbs, garlic, and ^{1}/$_3$ cup olive oil. Stir to blend and set aside.

Clean the mushrooms with a damp cloth. Cut them into ^{1}/$_2$-inch-thick slices and brush them lightly with olive oil. Place on the grill and cook for 3 minutes on each side, or until lightly browned.

Transfer to a serving platter and brush with the herb-oil mixture. Serve at once.

SERVES 4 TO 6

Fagioli al Fiasco
BAKED BEANS

In the past, dishes were often left to cook while people went out to work the fields. Fagioli al fiasco was one of those dishes, beans left to simmer for hours in the coals of the kitchen fire. The container was a heavy green hand-blown glass bottle known as a fiasco. Into the bottle went beans, water, garlic, olive oil, salt, and fresh herbs (usually sage). The bottle would be closed with a cloth, then covered with coals and ash and left for hours. Today, the same dish is made in a Dutch oven or other ovenproof casserole and baked in the oven.

1 cup dried cannellini beans, rinsed and picked over

2 cloves garlic, gently smashed

3 fresh sage leaves

1/4 cup extra-virgin olive oil

1/2 teaspoon sea salt, plus more for seasoning

Freshly ground black pepper

In a medium saucepan, combine the beans, garlic, and sage. Add water to cover by 2 inches and soak overnight.

Preheat the oven to 350°F. Drain the beans and place them in an ovenproof casserole dish. Add water to cover by 1 inch. Add the olive oil and 1/2 teaspoon salt, cover, and bake for 2 hours, or until the beans are tender. Season to taste with salt and pepper.

SERVES 4

Fagioli Cannellini
COOKED CANNELLINI BEANS

True Italian cannellini beans can be found in the resources (see page 177). Most cannellini beans in the U.S. market, even in gourmet stores, are white kidney beans grown in the Americas. They can be substituted, but the Italian bean is sweeter and has a wonderful creamy but firm consistency when cooked.

1 cup dried cannellini beans, rinsed and picked over

2 cloves garlic, gently smashed

3 fresh sage leaves

1/4 cup extra-virgin olive oil

1/2 teaspoon sea salt

In a medium saucepan, combine the beans, garlic, and sage. Add water to cover by 2 inches and soak overnight.

Drain the beans and place them in a large stockpot with the garlic and sage. Add water to cover by 1 inch. Add the olive oil and salt, cover, and bring to a boil. Skim any foam and decrease the heat to a simmer. Cover and cook for 2 hours, or until tender, adding water as needed to keep the beans moist as they cook.

MAKES 3 CUPS

Zucca al Forno
BAKED WINTER SQUASH

October and November are the peak of the season for winter squash, though it can be kept for months longer. Besides pairing perfectly with roasted or grilled meats, the roasted squash can be cooled and puréed to use later as a ravioli filling.

1 1/2 pounds acorn squash or butternut squash, peeled, halved, and seeded

3 tablespoons extra-virgin olive oil

Sea salt and freshly ground black pepper

Preheat an oven to 375°F. Lightly oil a baking dish.

Cut the squash into 1-inch-thick slices, and place them in the prepared dish in a single layer. Drizzle with the olive oil, season with salt and pepper to taste, and bake for 35 to 40 minutes, or until fork-tender. Serve at once.

SERVES 4

Pomodori, Fagioli, e Cipolline

ROASTED TOMATOES, BEANS, AND ONIONS

This hearty vegetable casserole needs no meat to make a satisfying meal on a cold night. If the small, squat onions known as cipolline are not available, you can substitute 4 quartered sweet red onions or 4 heads of garlic with the tops removed.

2 pounds potatoes, peeled and cut into
    2-inch pieces

2 pounds cipolline onions, about 1 1/2 inches
    in diameter, trimmed and peeled

1 bulb fennel, cored and cut lengthwise
    into eighths

1/4 cup extra-virgin olive oil

Sea salt and freshly ground black pepper
    to taste

2 cups cherry tomatoes

3 cups cooked cannellini beans (page 133)

3 sprigs fresh thyme for garnish

Preheat the oven to 400°F. Place the potatoes, onions, and fennel in a roasting pan. Add the olive oil and toss well to coat. Season with salt and pepper to taste. Roast, turning occasionally, for 20 minutes. Add the tomatoes and roast another 10 to 15 minutes, or until the potatoes and cipolline are fork-tender and golden brown. Add the beans, garnish with thyme, and serve at once.

SERVES 8 TO 10

Uova ai Piselli alla Marelia

Marelia's Peas and Eggs

Maria Aurelia Oriente's memories of the wartime cuisine revolve around peas (see page 23). They were eaten fresh in season and dried the rest of the year. She still prepares them, and this is still one of her favorite dishes. If you're serving a crowd, use a casserole dish rather than individual ramekins. The cooking time is the same. Frozen peas can be substituted when fresh peas are not in season.

1/4 cup extra-virgin olive oil

1 onion, finely chopped

2 ounces pancetta, diced

1 cup water

1 pound fresh or frozen green peas

4 large eggs

Sea salt and freshly ground black pepper

Preheat an oven to 375°F. Lightly oil four 1-cup ramekins.

In a large saucepan, heat the olive oil over medium-high heat, and sauté the onion and pancetta for 2 to 3 minutes, or until softened but not browned. Add the water and bring to a boil. Add the peas, decrease the heat to a brisk simmer, and cook for 3 minutes. Drain the peas and divide them among the prepared ramekins. Make a well in the center of each cup of peas and crack an egg into the well. Season with salt and pepper to taste, cover with aluminum foil, and place on a baking sheet. Bake for 12 to 14 minutes, or until the egg white is completely set. Serve at once.

Serves 4

Ceci Stufati
STEWED CHICKPEAS

In the area around Pisa, chickpeas are stewed with greens and anchovies, a delightful combination. Pasta can also be added for a complete one-dish meal.

1 cup dried chickpeas, rinsed and picked over

1/2 cup extra-virgin olive oil

1 onion, finely chopped

2 carrots, peeled and finely chopped

1 stalk celery, finely chopped

6 cups water, heated

3 ripe tomatoes, peeled, seeded, and coarsely chopped (see page 175)

3 salt-cured anchovies, rinsed and mashed

8 ounces Swiss chard, shredded

Sea salt and freshly ground black pepper

Place the chickpeas in a medium saucepan, and add water to cover by 2 inches. Soak overnight.

Drain the chickpeas. In a large, heavy saucepan, heat the olive oil over medium-high heat. Add the onion, carrots, and celery, and cook for 4 to 5 minutes, or until the onion is golden. Add the water, tomatoes, anchovies, and drained chickpeas. Bring to a boil, then decrease the heat to a simmer, cover, and cook for 1 1/2 hours. Add the chard and cook for another 30 minutes, or until the chickpeas are tender. Season to taste with salt and pepper.

SERVES 4

Cicoria in Padella

SAUTÉED WILD GREENS

In the past, the cicoria, or chicory, in this recipe was a wild green also called puntarelle. *Belgian endive and red radicchio are also members of the chicory family, with the characteristic bitter taste that complements fatty dishes. Arugula is a good substitute if you can't find the greens listed in this recipe. Delicious as a side dish, these sautéed greens are also an excellent topping for bruschetta or tossed with pasta.*

2 pounds wild chicory, dandelion greens, and/or nettles

1/4 cup extra-virgin olive oil, plus more for drizzling

1/2 cup chopped onion

2 anchovy fillets

Sea salt and freshly ground black pepper

In a large pot of salted boiling water, cook the greens for 10 minutes. Drain, let cool to the touch, and squeeze small handfuls to remove excess water. Set aside.

In a large sauté pan, heat the 1/4 cup olive oil over medium heat and sauté the onion and anchovies for 2 to 3 minutes, or until the onion is softened. Add the cooked greens, tossing to coat them. Season with salt and pepper to taste. Transfer to a serving dish, drizzle with olive oil, and serve at once.

SERVES 4

Fanne meno e condiscila meglio.

Make less and dress it better.

Bread & Sweets

Schiacciata all'Uva

GRAPE FOCACCIA

Schiacciata means "flattened" and is the local Tuscan name for the flat bread known as focaccia in other areas. In the fall, when the grapes are being harvested, it is made with grapes. Some versions contain rosemary, some use milk, and some have egg; some mix the grapes in the dough, and some put the grapes on top—but all of them use grapes with seeds for the added crunch.

1 tablespoon active dry yeast, or 1 ounce
    fresh cake yeast

3 cups warm water (105° to 115°F)

1/2 cup sugar, plus more for sprinkling

7 to 8 cups unbleached all-purpose flour

1 cup coarsely chopped walnuts, plus
    1/2 cup walnut halves

1 teaspoon sea salt

1 pound Sangiovese grapes (or your
    favorite local variety)

2 tablespoons extra-virgin olive oil

In a large bowl, stir the yeast into the warm water until it dissolves. Add the 1/2 cup sugar, 1 cup of the flour, the chopped walnuts, and salt and stir to mix well. One cup at a time, stir in as much of the remaining flour as needed to make a workable dough. Transfer to a floured work surface, and knead for 10 to 15 minutes, or until smooth and elastic, adding tablespoonfuls of the remaining flour as needed.

Shape the dough into a ball, and put in a lightly oiled bowl. Turn the ball to coat it with oil. Cover with a damp towel or plastic wrap, and let rise in a warm, draft-free place for 1 hour, or until doubled in volume.

Lightly oil a baking sheet. Punch down the dough and place it in the prepared pan. Press and push the dough into the edges of the pan. Brush with the olive oil, and press the grapes and walnut halves into the dough. Sprinkle with sugar and let rise for 45 minutes, or until doubled in height.

Preheat the oven to 400°F. Bake for 30 minutes, or until golden. Let cool to room temperature and cut into squares to serve.

MAKES 1 FLAT BREAD; SERVES 12

Pane Sciocco Toscano

Unsalted Tuscan Bread

Many of the classic Tuscan recipes were born from a need to use up dry or day-old bread. Since Tuscan bread was made only once a week and was made without salt, which helps keep bread moist, it dried out quickly. Salt was expensive for the peasant farmer as it was heavily taxed, and he used it only for the things that were essential, such as curing meats and making cheese.

The recipe below was inspired by two of my colleagues, Nancy Harmon Jenkins and Carol Field. We all agree that a truly traditional Tuscan bread should be made with stone-ground flour and good water. It should be fermented slowly, and ideally should be baked in a wood-fired oven. A pizza stone in a regular oven is a good alternative.

A slow fermentation is best, using a starter. If you live near a winery you can make a natural starter: Simply leave a slurry of equal parts of flour and water in the fermentation room overnight, and wild yeasts from the fermenting grapes will start to grow in the mixture.

The following starter can be made in your own kitchen. To keep a continuous source of starter, make a double batch of this recipe, then take half of it out before continuing on to make the bread as directed. The reserved starter should be refrigerated in an airtight container and used within 10 to 14 days, or be fed once a week by stirring in 1/2 cup warm water and 1 cup of flour. To bake later, let the starter warm to room temperature and proceed with the bread recipe.

Day 1: Making the Starter

1 teaspoon active dry yeast

1 cup warm spring water (105° to 115°F)

2 cups unbleached all-purpose flour

In a large bowl, stir the yeast into the warm water until it dissolves. Gradually whisk in the flour until blended. Cover with plastic wrap and let stand in a cool place for at least 8 hours or overnight.

Day 2: Making the Starter Dough

2 cups unbleached all-purpose flour

1 cup warm spring water (105° to 115°F)

Starter from Day 1 (see page 148)

Stir the flour and water into the starter until blended. Cover with plastic wrap and let stand in a cool place for at least 8 hours or as long as overnight.

(recipe continued on page 148)

Pane Sciocco Toscano *(continued)*

DAY 3: MAKING THE BREAD

2 cups warm spring water (105° to 115°F)

6 to 7 cups unbleached all-purpose flour

Starter Dough from Day 2 (see page 147)

Cornmeal for pizza paddle

Add the water and 1 cup of the flour to the starter dough and stir until blended. Continue stirring in 1 cup of flour at a time until a workable dough is formed. Transfer the dough to a floured board, and knead for 10 to 15 minutes, or until smooth and elastic, adding tablespoonfuls of flour as needed to prevent sticking.

Shape the dough into a ball and place it in a lightly oiled bowl. Turn the ball to coat it with oil. Cover with a damp towel or plastic wrap, and let rise in a warm, draft-free place until doubled in volume; because of the slow-rising starter, this may take 2 hours or longer.

Punch down the dough and turn it out onto a lightly floured work surface. Knead lightly and shape into a large round loaf. Place the loaf on a pizza paddle or rimless baking sheet that has been sprinkled with cornmeal. The cornmeal will act as little ball bearings to help slide the loaf into the oven later. Cover with a damp towel, then let it rise for 1 hour.

Preheat an oven, with a pizza stone inside, to 475°F. Score the top of the loaf with a razor blade or sharp knife in a crosshatch design, and slide the loaf onto the preheated pizza stone. Bake for 10 minutes, then decrease the heat to 375°F. Bake for 30 minutes longer, or until the bread is golden brown.

MAKES 1 LARGE LOAF OR 2 MEDIUM LOAVES

Sfratti
Walnut and Honey Bars

Sfratti, a sweet served at Rosh Hashanah, is one of the old recipes of Pitigliano (see page 28) that has been recognized by Slow Food (www.slowfood.com) as an important Italian-Jewish tradition. The sfratto is a thin layer of unleavened dough filled with honey, walnuts, orange zest, and nutmeg and baked. Shaped like a large cigar, it recalls the batons officials used to bang on the doors of Jews to evict them. The word sfratto means "eviction."

Pastry

3 cups unbleached all-purpose flour

1 cup sugar

Pinch of salt

1/3 cup extra-virgin olive oil

2/3 cup sweet white wine

Filling

1 cup honey

4 cups walnuts, chopped

2 teaspoons grated orange zest

1 teaspoon ground cinnamon

1/2 teaspoon ground cloves

1 egg yolk, beaten

For the pastry: In a large bowl, combine the flour, sugar, and salt. Stir with a whisk to blend. Stir in the olive oil and wine to make a smooth dough. Wrap in plastic wrap and refrigerate for at least 1 hour or overnight.

Preheat the oven to 350°F. Line a baking sheet with parchment paper.

For the filling: In a medium saucepan, heat the honey over medium heat. Add the walnuts, orange zest, cinnamon, and cloves, and cook, stirring constantly, for 5 minutes, or until thickened. Remove from the heat and let cool slightly.

Divide the chilled dough into 8 pieces. On a lightly floured work surface, roll a piece of dough into a 4 by 10-inch rectangle. Spoon 1/2 cup of the filling along the center of the length of the dough and roll it up. Place on the prepared baking sheet, seam side down. Repeat with the remaining pastry and filling. Brush the pastry with the egg yolk, and bake for 20 minutes, or until golden brown.

Transfer the pastries from the pan to a wire rack to cool completely. To serve, cut each pastry into 1-inch-thick slices. Store in an airtight container for up to 3 weeks.

Makes about 6 dozen slices

Crostate di Prugne

PLUM JAM TART

Our local prune plums are called cosce di monache, or nuns' thighs. Could it be because they are so sweet? I make a simple jam with them in July when it seems like it's raining plums: two-thirds pitted plums to one-third sugar by weight, cooked until quite thick, then puréed with a food mill. Any thick jam or preserves can be used in this tart. The short pastry crust is known as pasta frolla in Italy.

SHORT PASTRY CRUST

4 1/2 cups unbleached all-purpose flour

2 cups sugar

Pinch of salt

1/2 teaspoon baking powder

1/2 teaspoon baking soda

1 pound cold unsalted butter, cut into
    small pieces

5 large eggs

Grated zest of 1 lemon

1/2 teaspoon vanilla extract

1 1/4 cups plum jam or your favorite flavor

1 egg yolk beaten with 1 tablespoon water

1 tablespoon granulated sugar

For the crust: In a large bowl, combine the flour, sugar, salt, baking powder, and baking soda. Stir with a whisk to blend. Using your fingertips or a pastry cutter, work or cut the butter pieces into the flour mixture to form pea-sized crumbs.

In a medium bowl, combine the eggs, lemon zest, and vanilla. Whisk to blend well. With a fork, stir the eggs into the flour mixture, blending just until incorporated. Transfer to a lightly floured work surface, and press the dough gently into a smooth rectangle about 10 by 12 inches. Wrap in plastic and refrigerate for at least 1 hour or up to 24 hours.

Preheat the oven to 350°F. Line a baking sheet with parchment paper.

(recipe continued on page 152)

Crostate di Prugne (continued)

On a lightly floured work surface, roll two-thirds of the dough out to a 12 by 15-inch rectangle. Transfer it to the prepared pan, and spread the jam evenly over the pastry, leaving a 1/2-inch border.

Roll out the remaining dough and cut into 1/2-inch-wide strips. Crisscross the strips diagonally on the top of the tart, making a lattice design. Brush the lattice with the egg yolk mixture and sprinkle with the granulated sugar. Bake for 40 to 50 minutes, or until the crust is golden. Let cool completely and cut into squares to serve.

MAKES I (12 BY 15-INCH) TART; SERVES 8

Torta di Ricotta

RICOTTA CAKE

This is a simple dessert, moist with ricotta cheese and fragrant with lemon zest. Like most Italian desserts, it is very lightly sweetened. Ricotta is actually a by-product of the cheese-making process. Once the curd has been removed to age and become cheese, the liquid that is left (the whey) is recooked, which is what the Italian word ricotta means. The heated whey thickens and becomes a creamy delicacy. If you don't have a cheesemaker nearby, look for fresh whole-milk ricotta from a cheese shop, natural food store, or gourmet market; it will have more flavor than other ricottas.

3 large eggs, separated

1/2 cup sugar

1 1/4 cups (10 ounces) whole-milk ricotta cheese

1/3 cup whole milk

Grated zest of 2 lemons

Pinch of salt

1 1/2 cups unbleached all-purpose flour

1 1/2 teaspoons baking powder

Powdered sugar for dusting

Preheat the oven to 375°F. Liberally butter and lightly flour a 9-inch springform pan; knock out the excess flour.

In a large bowl, combine the egg yolks and sugar, and beat until light and creamy. Stir in the ricotta, milk, lemon zest, and salt. In a medium bowl, combine the flour and baking powder, and stir with a whisk to blend. Add the flour mixture to the ricotta mixture, stirring just enough to mix.

In a large bowl, beat the egg whites until soft peaks form. Using a rubber spatula, stir one-third of the beaten whites into the batter, then carefully fold in the remaining whites until blended.

Scrape the batter into the prepared pan and smooth the top. Bake for 35 minutes, or until a toothpick inserted in the center comes out clean and the cake pulls away from the sides of the pan. Let cool completely, then loosen the edges with a thin-bladed knife and release the sides of the springform pan. Dust with powdered sugar and cut into wedges to serve.

MAKES 1 (9-INCH) CAKE; SERVES 8

Castagnaccio
CHESTNUT CAKE

This dense cake is an acquired taste, and it has taken me almost twenty years to acquire it. But its musky chewiness is much loved by Tuscans. The version below is from Renza del Bianco (see page 22). I sometimes add raisins, and I love it topped with fresh ricotta and chestnut honey. The cake can also be made with walnuts instead of pine nuts.

Olive oil and dried bread crumbs or flour
   for cake pan

5 cups chestnut flour

$^1/_2$ cup sugar

Pinch of salt

3 cups water

3 tablespoons extra-virgin olive oil

Grated zest of 1 lemon

$^1/_4$ cup pine nuts, toasted (see page 175)

1 cup whole-milk ricotta, preferably
   sheep's milk, for serving

Preheat the oven to 375°F. Grease a 10-inch springform pan with olive oil and dust it with bread crumbs; tap out the excess.

In a large bowl, combine the chestnut flour, sugar, and salt. Stir with a whisk to blend, then stir in the water, olive oil, and lemon zest to make a thin batter like pancake batter. Pour into the prepared pan. Sprinkle the pine nuts over the batter and bake for 35 to 40 minutes, or until a toothpick inserted in the center comes out clean.

Transfer to a wire rack and let cool completely. Remove the sides of the pan, cut the cake into wedges, and serve topped with a dollop of ricotta cheese.

MAKES 1 (10-INCH) CAKE; SERVES 6

Ciambellone

Tuscan Ring Cake

Our family often goes to the tiny Trattoria Tripolitania in Sarteano on Saturday nights for honest homemade food. This simple cake made by the owner/cook Franca Magi makes our adopted grandpa, Virio Neri, swoon with memories of his childhood. "My mother used to bake this cake with a can in the middle to form the hole," reminisces Virio. When speaking of times past, Franca expresses a sentiment that I heard from many people. "We had less, but we were better off; the food was poco, ma buono, simple and full of flavor. We appreciated what we had more because it was harder to come by."

5 cups unbleached all-purpose flour

1 1/2 teaspoons baking powder

Pinch of salt

5 large eggs

2 1/2 cups sugar

1 cup milk

1 cup extra-virgin olive oil

Grated zest and juice of 1 lemon

Preheat the oven to 400°F. Lightly butter and flour a 12-inch tube pan; knock out the excess flour.

In a medium bowl, combine the flour, baking powder, and salt. Stir with a whisk to blend. Set aside.

In another bowl, whisk the eggs until blended, then gradually whisk in the sugar. Stir in the milk, olive oil, lemon zest, and lemon juice. Fold in the flour mixture just until blended.

Pour the batter into the prepared pan and smooth the top. Bake for 40 to 45 minutes, or until the top is golden and the cake pulls away from the sides of the pan. Remove from the oven, invert on a cake rack, and let cool completely. Run a thin knife around the sides of the pan and invert the cake onto a plate. Cut into wedges to serve.

MAKES 1 (10-INCH) TUBE CAKE; SERVES 8

Scarpaccia
Zucchini Cake

*Renza del Bianco (see page 22) shared this recipe,
which falls between a sweet and a savory dish, and
is a typical dessert from the Versilia coast. It's ideal
to make in summer when the zucchini harvest is in.*

Olive oil and dried bread crumbs or
    flour for pan

1 1/3 cups unbleached all-purpose flour

1 1/3 cups sugar

2 large eggs, beaten

1/4 cup extra-virgin olive oil

Pinch of salt

6 to 8 leaves fresh basil, minced

1 pound zucchini, thinly sliced crosswise

Preheat the oven to 375°F. Lightly oil a 10-inch
springform pan and dust it with bread crumbs;
knock out the excess.

In a large bowl, combine the flour, sugar, eggs, olive
oil, basil, and salt. Stir until well blended. Add the
zucchini and stir well. Scrape into the prepared pan
and smooth the top.

Bake for 45 minutes, or until the edges pull away
from the sides of the pan and a knife inserted in
the center comes out clean. Let cool completely on
a wire rack. Cut into wedges to serve.

Makes 1 (10-inch) cake; serves 10 to 12

Cenci

Fried Carnival Sweets

Lucia Giovanna Puccetti of Pietrasanta shared her recipe for this fried pastry. Made at carnival time, it goes by many names: chiacchere ("gossips"), nastrini ("ribbons"), and cenci or stracci ("rags"). The shapes vary from bowties to diamonds to simple strips. These are best when first made, but can be kept for a few days in an airtight container.

⅓ cup granulated sugar

4 large eggs

4 tablespoons unsalted butter, softened

1 cup sparkling water, dry white wine, or vin santo

Grated zest of 1 lemon

Pinch of salt

3 cups unbleached all-purpose flour

Canola oil for deep-frying

Powdered sugar for dusting

In a large bowl, combine the granulated sugar, eggs, and butter. Beat with a wooden spoon or electric mixer until creamy. Stir in the sparkling water, lemon zest, and salt. Stir in the flour, blending to a stiff dough. Cover and refrigerate for 1 hour.

On a lightly floured work surface, roll the dough out to a thickness of ⅛ inch. Using a fluted pastry wheel, cut the dough into 1 by 3-inch strips. Make a cut down the center of each strip, leaving the ends attached.

In a deep, heavy pot, heat 3 inches of oil to 375°F on a deep-fat thermometer. Working in batches, fry the pastry for about 3 to 4 minutes, or until golden. Using a wire skimmer, transfer to paper towels to drain. Transfer to a baking sheet and let cool completely. Dust with powdered sugar.

Makes about 3 dozen *cenci*

Cantucci

ALMOND BISCOTTI

The word biscotti literally means "twice-cooked," as these hard cookies are first baked in a loaf, then sliced and baked again. The classic Tuscan biscotti known as cantucci will keep nearly forever in an airtight container, and are splendid dipped in sweet wine or coffee.

1 3/4 cups cake flour

1 cup unbleached all-purpose flour

1 teaspoon sea salt

1 teaspoon baking powder

1/2 teaspoon baking soda

1 cup unblanched almonds, toasted
   (page 175)

4 large eggs

3/4 cup sugar

2 teaspoons vanilla extract

1 tablespoon grated orange zest

Preheat the oven to 325°F. Line a baking sheet with parchment paper.

In a large bowl, combine the cake flour, all-purpose flour, salt, baking powder, and baking soda. Stir with a whisk to blend. Stir in the almonds.

In a medium bowl, beat the eggs and sugar together until pale in color. Stir in the vanilla and orange zest. Stir the egg mixture into the dry ingredients just until blended. Do not overmix. The dough will be sticky.

Moisten your fingers with water and transfer the dough to the prepared pan, forming a log about 3 inches wide. Bake for about 30 minutes, or until a toothpick inserted into the center comes out clean. Transfer to a wire rack and let cool slightly. Decrease the oven temperature to 275°F. Replace the parchment paper on the baking sheet.

Using a large, sharp knife, cut the log crosswise into 1/2-inch-thick slices on the diagonal. Place the slices on the prepared pan and bake for about 20 minutes, or until a pale golden brown, about 20 minutes. Transfer to wire racks to cool completely. Store in an airtight container for up to 6 weeks.

MAKES ABOUT 2 DOZEN COOKIES

*Clockwise from top, center: Cantucci,
Ricciarelli, Brutti Ma Buoni, Cavallucci*

Ricciarelli
SIENESE ALMOND COOKIES

When I think of Siena, I think of these cookies.
They are too rich to have been part of the daily
diet in hard times, but they could have been a special
treat for farms with an almond tree. The original
recipe is quite lengthy, taking days to prepare, but I
think my simplified version is reasonable.

1 cup (6 ounces) blanched almonds

1 cup granulated sugar

3 tablespoons unbleached all-purpose flour

3/4 teaspoon baking powder

1 tablespoon finely grated orange zest

4 large egg whites

1/8 teaspoon almond extract

1/2 cup powdered sugar, sifted, for coating

Preheat the oven to 350°F. Line two baking sheets with parchment paper.

In a food processor, place the almonds, 3/4 cup granulated sugar, and flour; process to a fine powder. Add the baking powder and orange zest. Pulse to blend well.

In a large bowl, beat the egg whites until stiff, gradually adding the remaining 1/4 cup sugar, beating until glossy peaks form. Add the almond extract.

Remove the almond mixture from the food processor and place in a large bowl. Stir one-third of the egg white mixture into the almond mixture to lighten it, then carefully fold in the rest of the egg white mixture with a rubber spatula.

Drop tablespoonfuls of batter 2 inches apart onto the prepared pan and dust liberally with the powdered sugar. Bake for 12 to 15 minutes, or until lightly golden and firm to the touch. Let cool on the pan for 10 minutes before transferring to a wire rack to cool completely. Store in an airtight container for up to 6 weeks.

MAKES ABOUT 2 DOZEN COOKIES

Brutti Ma Buoni

UGLY BUT GOOD COOKIES

Although it seems counterproductive in this recipe to beat the egg whites and then cook them, the beating process changes the composition of the batter and gives the cookies their unique chewy character. This basic recipe can be varied by adding lemon or orange zest, powdered cocoa, or a splash of Frangelico (hazelnut liqueur) to the nut mixture. In place of almonds or hazelnuts, you can use pine nuts or walnuts.

2 cups blanched almonds, toasted (page 175), or hazelnuts, toasted and skinned (page 175)

1/4 cup granulated sugar

1/4 teaspoon ground cinnamon

A few gratings of nutmeg

4 large egg whites at room temperature

Pinch of salt

3/4 cup superfine sugar

Preheat the oven to 325°F. Line a baking sheet with parchment paper.

In a food processor, combine the nuts, granulated sugar, cinnamon, and nutmeg. Pulse to a coarse meal. Set aside.

In a large bowl, beat the egg whites and salt until soft peaks form. Gradually beat in the superfine sugar, 1 tablespoon at a time, until all the sugar has been added and stiff, glossy peaks form.

Using a rubber spatula, fold the egg whites into the nut mixture, and transfer the batter to a medium saucepan. Cook over low heat, stirring constantly, for about 20 minutes, or until the batter thickens and turns a light golden color.

Drop teaspoonfuls of batter 2 inches apart onto the prepared pan and bake for 30 minutes, or until dry on the outside and firm to the touch. Transfer the cookies from the pan to a wire rack to cool completely. Store in an airtight container for up to 6 weeks.

MAKES ABOUT 2 DOZEN COOKIES

Cavallucci

SIENESE HORSE COOKIES

Siena has made these anise-flavored cookies since the Renaissance. I would guess that the name has something to do with the Palio horse race, even though historians say it is because they were originally made for the men who worked in the stables.

1 ³/₄ cups granulated sugar

³/₄ cup water

2 tablespoons honey

4 cups unbleached all-purpose flour

1 tablespoon aniseeds

1 ¹/₂ teaspoons baking powder

Powdered sugar for coating

In a small saucepan, combine the granulated sugar, water, and honey. Bring to a simmer over medium heat and cook, stirring constantly, until thickened, about 15 minutes.

In a large bowl, combine the flour, aniseeds, and baking powder. Stir in the sugar mixture until blended to make a fairly stiff dough. Cover and refrigerate for 30 minutes.

Preheat the oven to 325°F. Line a baking sheet with parchment paper.

Roll heaping teaspoonfuls of the dough into 1-inch-diameter balls. Roll each in powdered sugar to coat, and place on the prepared pan 2 inches apart. Bake for 8 to 10 minutes, or until lightly browned. Transfer from the pan to a wire rack and let cool completely. Store up to 6 weeks in an airtight container.

MAKES ABOUT 3 DOZEN COOKIES

Biscotti dei Poveri

PEASANT COOKIES

*As their name implies, these cookies are made with
simple ingredients and use dry or day-old bread in
place of flour. You can also embellish them with more
nuts, vanilla extract, or grated orange zest.*

8 ounces dry or day-old bread

2 cups whole milk, warmed

3 eggs

1 cup sugar

1/4 cup extra-virgin olive oil

1/2 cup pine nuts

1/2 cup raisins

1/2 teaspoon cinnamon

Tear or cut the bread into pieces and place in a large
bowl. Cover with the milk and set aside for an hour
or so until the bread is softened.

Preheat the oven to 375°F. Line a baking sheet with
parchment paper.

Place the softened bread in a food processor and
puree until smooth. In a large bowl, beat the eggs
and sugar for 5 minutes, until thick and creamy. Add
the olive oil, pine nuts, raisins, cinnamon, and soaked
bread. Mix well. Drop the batter by tablespoonfuls
onto the prepared pan. Bake for 8 to 10 minutes,
or until golden. Transfer to a wire rack to cool
completely. Store in an airtight container for up
to 2 weeks.

MAKES ABOUT 3 DOZEN COOKIES

Fichi allo Virio
VIRIO'S STUFFED FIGS

Virio is our adopted Italian grandfather, the cobbler of Montepulciano. He grew up there during World War II and remembers times of hunger and deprivation. But when he starts to talk about what his family ate, even though food was scarce, his memories are rich and include the stuffed figs his mother made every September. Hers were stuffed simply with walnuts and put into the wood-burning stove to melt to a juicy treat. This adaptation adds some creamy cheese.

12 ripe figs

12 walnut halves

2 ounces Gorgonzola cheese

12 fig leaves, optional

Preheat the oven to 375°F. Lightly oil a 8-inch cake pan.

Cut a lengthwise slit in each fig. Insert a half walnut and a marble-sized piece of cheese. Close and place in the prepared cake pan. Cover lightly with aluminum foil and bake for 10 minutes, or until the cheese has melted and figs have softened.

VARIATION: If you have access to unsprayed fig leaves, place each stuffed fig on a fig leaf and wrap it like a package, tying it closed with string or raffia. Cook in a covered steamer over boiling water for 3 to 5 minutes. Don't leave longer or the leaf will begin to cook, which can cause an unpleasant odor.

SERVES 6

Mele al Forno

BAKED APPLES

*In September, I have a bountiful harvest of little
wild green apples from a tree in my garden. They
make wonderful baked apples to stuff with cookie
crumbs, spices, and sugar. Granny Smith apples
would work well here.*

6 Cantucci (page 162), Brutti Ma Buoni (page 165),
   or purchased amaretti cookies

6 tablespoons sugar

Grated zest of 1 orange

1 teaspoon ground cinnamon

A few gratings of nutmeg

6 tablespoons unsalted butter, softened

3 Granny Smith apples, halved horizontally

Preheat the oven to 350°F. Lightly butter a casserole
dish big enough to hold 6 apple halves.

In a food processor, combine the cookies, sugar,
orange zest, cinnamon, and nutmeg, and pulse to a
coarse meal. Remove half of the mixture and reserve.
Add the butter to the remaining mixture in the food
processor and pulse to make a creamy filling.

Using a melon baller, scoop out the apple cores, taking
care not to break through the sides or bottoms. Place
the apples in the prepared dish, cut side up. Scoop a
heaping teaspoonful of the filling mixture into each
apple. Sprinkle the reserved crumb mixture over the
top. Cover the casserole with aluminum foil, making
sure it doesn't touch the apples, and bake for 20 to
25 minutes, or until the apples are soft. Serve warm.

SERVES 6

Basics

Vegetable Stock

¹/₄ cup extra-virgin olive oil

2 onions, coarsely chopped

2 carrots, peeled and coarsely chopped

3 stalks celery, coarsely chopped

¹/₂ cup dry white wine

1 gallon (4 quarts) spring water

Bouquet garni: 1 sprig parsley, 1 sprig thyme,
    1 bay leaf, 4 or 5 black peppercorns, tied in
    a square of cheesecloth

In a large stockpot, heat the olive oil over
medium heat and sauté the onions, carrots,
and celery for 5 to 8 minutes, or until browned.
Add the wine, increase the heat to high, and stir
to scrape up the browned bits from the bottom
of the pan. Continue cooking until the wine is
almost completely evaporated. Add the water
and bouquet garni. Bring to a boil, decrease
the heat to a simmer, and cook, uncovered, for
45 minutes. Strain the stock and discard the
vegetables. Cover and store in the refrigerator
for up to 3 days, or freeze for up to 3 months.

MAKES 12 CUPS

Meat Stock

6 pounds beef or veal shank bones, cut into
    3-inch lengths

2 onions, cut into 1-inch pieces

Olive oil for coating

2 carrots, peeled and cut into 1-inch pieces

1 stalk celery, cut into 1-inch pieces

Bouquet garni: 1 sprig parsley, 1 sprig thyme,
    1 bay leaf, and 4 or 5 peppercorns, tied in a
    cheesecloth square

10 quarts water

Preheat the oven to 425°F. Lightly oil a roasting
pan and add the bones and onions. Roast, turning
occasionally, until very brown, 35 to 40 minutes.

In a large stockpot, combine the bones, onions,
and all the remaining ingredients and bring to
a boil. Skim the foam from the top. Decrease
the heat to medium and simmer, uncovered, for
3 hours, skimming the foam occasionally.

Strain the stock into another container and
discard the solids. Let cool, cover, and refrigerate
overnight. Remove the congealed fat. Store in
the refrigerator for up to 3 days, or freeze for up
to 3 months.

MAKES 5 QUARTS

Chicken Stock

1 (3-pound) chicken, cut up

1 carrot, peeled and cut into $1/2$-inch pieces

1 stalk celery, cut into $1/2$-inch pieces

1 onion, cut into $1/2$-inch pieces

Bouquet garni: 1 sprig parsley, 1 sprig thyme,
    1 bay leaf, and 4 or 5 peppercorns, tied in a
    cheesecloth square

1 gallon (4 quarts) water

In a large stockpot, combine all the ingredients
and bring to a boil. Decrease the heat to a simmer
and skim off the foam. Simmer, uncovered, for
2 hours, skimming occasionally. Strain the stock
into another container and discard the solids. Let
cool, cover, and refrigerate the stock overnight.
Remove the congealed fat. Store in the refrigerator for up to 3 days, or freeze for up to 3 months.

MAKES 3 QUARTS

Tomato Sauce

3 tablespoons extra-virgin olive oil

1 small onion, coarsely chopped

2 pounds tomatoes, peeled, seeded, and
    coarsely chopped (see page 175)

2 cloves garlic

$1/4$ cup minced fresh flat-leaf parsley

1 tablespoon minced fresh basil

Sea salt and freshly ground black pepper

In a large sauté pan, heat the olive oil over
medium-high heat, and sauté the onion for 2 to
3 minutes, or until softened. Add the tomatoes,
garlic, parsley, and basil. Decrease the heat to
low and cook uncovered, stirring occasionally,
for 20 minutes. Pass the mixture through a food
mill or purée in a blender until smooth. Season
with salt and pepper to taste.

MAKES 6 CUPS

Pasta Dough

3 cups unbleached all-purpose flour

4 large eggs

1 tablespoon safflower oil

Place the flour in a food processor. In a 16-ounce glass measuring cup, whisk the eggs with the oil. With the machine running, gradually add the egg mixture and process until the dough starts to come away from the sides of the work bowl. Process for 30 seconds longer and check the consistency. The dough should be moist enough to pinch together, but not sticky.

On a lightly floured work surface, knead the dough into a ball. Transfer to a zip-top plastic bag, and let rest for at least 30 minutes.

Divide the dough into 4 pieces, and reserve 3 pieces in the closed plastic bag. Form the fourth piece into a rectangle. Using a hand-cranked pasta machine on the widest setting, run the rectangle of dough, beginning with one of the shorter sides, through the machine. Fold the dough in half and put it through the machine again. Repeat 8 to 10 times, or until the dough is smooth. If the dough tears, it may be too wet; dust it with flour, brushing off the excess.

Adjust the pasta machine to the next narrower setting. Continue putting the dough through the rollers, without folding it, using a narrower setting each time, until the dough is the desired thinness. Allow the rolled dough to dry while rolling each remaining piece of dough, then cut the sheets into the desired pasta shape.

HANDMADE PASTA: Mound the flour on a work surface. Make a well in the center and add the eggs and oil. Using a fork, gradually blend the egg mixture into the flour. Clean and reflour the surface. Knead the dough, dusting with flour as needed, for 10 to 15 minutes, or until smooth and elastic. Transfer to a zip-top plastic bag, and let rest for at least 30 minutes.

MAKES 1 POUND

Toasting Nuts

Place the nuts on a baking sheet with sides, and toast in a preheated 350°F oven until golden brown and aromatic. Pine nuts will take 5 minutes; almonds and walnuts, 10 minutes.

Toasting and Skinning Hazelnuts

Place the nuts on a baking sheet with sides, and toast in a preheated 350°F oven until golden brown and aromatic, 12 to 15 minutes. Let cool, then place in a clean cotton towel and rub them together to peel them.

Peeling and Seeding Tomatoes

Cut the core from each tomato. Drop the tomatoes into boiling water for 30 seconds; using a wire skimmer or slotted spoon, immediately transfer to ice water to stop the cooking and release the skins. The peel will slip off in your hands. To seed, cut the tomatoes in half, invert each half over the sink, and squeeze out the seeds.

Steaming Spinach

Remove the stems from the spinach and rinse the leaves well. Place in a large saucepan over medium heat and cook for 2 to 3 minutes, or until wilted. Let cool, then squeeze by handfuls over the sink to remove as much moisture as possible.

Trimming Artichokes

To cut the artichokes into hearts, cut the stem close to the artichoke and remove the leaves by hand, starting at the base, until you reach the tender inner leaves. Continue pulling off the soft leaves until the fuzzy choke is exposed. Scrape out the choke with a spoon. Trim any remaining leaves with a sharp paring knife.

Acknowledgments

This has been a rich but difficult book to research—often heartbreaking. My initial reading of turn-of-the-century Italian life painted scenes that were meager and mean. After each reading, I found that I was very hungry. As I spoke with older people with memories of the "hard times," it soon became clear that those living now had suffered true difficulties during and after World War II. The stories that came forth were sad, bitter, and desperate. But even though nearly every single person said the same thing, "We had *nothing* to eat," the memories of the few foods that they did manage to survive on almost always evoked a pleasant memory.

Thank you for sharing: Virio Neri, Lina Mazzetti, Franca Magi, Ilvana Corsi Tognocchi, Ivano Leonardi, Renza del Bianco, Diana Menchini Puccetti, Lucia Giovanna Puccetti, Lucia Andreotti, Maria Aurelia Oriente, Anna Bessi, Eni Fiorini Marcucci, Meri Franceschi, Roberto Vitiello, Miriam Serni Casalini, Carlo Cioni, Maria Assunta Raffaelle, Ercolano Regoli, Giordano Andreucci, Sauro Petroni, and Evelina Modigliani Rossi.

Thank you for the introductions to family and friends: Simone and Enrico Agostinelli, Laura Bertuccelli, Andrea Bertucci, Marida Bessi, Rosanna Capitani, Kim and Dario Cecchini, Federica de Gori, Lina Mazzetti, Marco della

Rosa, Angelo Frati and the Chestnut Museum of Lucca, Serena Giovannoni, Andrea Leonardi, Anna Rita Merlini, Silvia Rossi, Antonella Vito, and Andrea Wyner.

Thank you to my literary colleague and friend Nancy Harmon Jenkins, for her shared expertise and the loan of some of her best books on food history. Thanks, also, to Lorenza de' Medici, Mary Ann Esposito, and Kyle Phillips, for their positive feedback.

For recipe testing and text feedback, my thanks to Kerry Allen, Jennifer Barry, Katherine Becker, Sandee Beckers, Pauline Behnke, Rolando Beramendi, Cathy Briles, Katherine Brownlee, Gail Casale, Amanda Cullen, Rachel Duboff, Philippa Farrar, Mary Laufer Francis, Wendy Grindstaff, Raleigh McDonald Hussung, Carolyn Kristina Kulik, Lucia Lahr, Sheila Lambert, Hill Leptich, Katherine Little, Deborah Mele, Angel Ratliff, Greg Robson, Janice Ross, Janine Bailey Sheldon, Sally and Michael Storm, Helen Sturgeon, and Julie Toft.

Thank you as always to my supportive and loving husband, Courtney Johns, and my fabulous teenager, Alaia Rose; to my collaborator, Jennifer Barry, the best book designer and friend around; to Carolyn Miller for her patient and careful editing; and to Andrea Wyner for the beautiful photography.

Resources

LEARN TO COOK IN ITALY
Italian Food Artisans, LLC
U.S. office: (805) 963-7289
www.FoodArtisans.com
E-mail: Pamela@FoodArtisans.com
Wine and food workshops with the author in several regions of Italy.

AGRITURISMO POGGIO ETRUSCO
Via del Pelago 11,
Loc. Fontecornino
53045 Montepulciano (SI)
(39) 0578 798 370
www.poggio-etrusco.com
E-mail: info@Poggio-Etrusco.com
Tuscan bed & breakfast and holiday rentals at the author's organic farm in Tuscany.

HERITAGE FOODS
402 Graham Avenue, Box 198
Brooklyn, NY 11211
(718) 389-0985
www.heritagefoodsusa.com
Supplier of heritage breeds of meats (including beef cheeks), poultry, and rabbit.

D'ARTAGNAN
(800) 327-8246
Fax (973) 465-1870
www.dartagnan.com
Game such as hare, boar, and duck; seasonal specialties such as mushrooms and truffles.

A. G. FERRARI
Catalog (877) 878-2783
www.agferrari.com
Imported artisanal Italian foods.

GUSTIAMO
(877) 907-2525
Fax (718) 860-4311
www.gustiamo.com
Imported artisanal Italian foods.

MANICARETTI
5332 College Avenue, No. 200
Oakland, CA 94618
(800) 799-9830
www.manicaretti.com
Imported artisanal Italian foods.

MARKET HALL FOODS
(888) 952-4005
Fax (510) 652-4669
www.markethallfoods.com
High-quality Italian pastas, oils, vinegars, cheeses, and spices.

NIMAN RANCH
(866) 808-0340
Fax (510) 808-0339
www.nimanranch.com
High-quality fresh and cured domestic meats.

SUR LA TABLE
Catalog (800) 243-0852
www.surlatable.com
Kitchen equipment and imported Italian foods.

WILLIAMS-SONOMA
Catalog (800) 541-2233
www.williams-sonoma.com
Kitchen equipment and imported Italian foods.

Metric Conversions & Equivalents

APPROXIMATE METRIC EQUIVALENTS

Volume

¹/₄ teaspoon	1 milliliter
¹/₂ teaspoon	2.5 milliliters
³/₄ teaspoon	4 milliliters
1 teaspoon	5 milliliters
1¹/₄ teaspoons	6 milliliters
1¹/₂ teaspoons	7.5 milliliters
1³/₄ teaspoons	8.5 milliliters
2 teaspoons	10 milliliters
1 tablespoon (¹/₂ fluid ounce)	15 milliliters
2 tablespoons (1 fluid ounce)	30 milliliters
¹/₄ cup	60 milliliters
¹/₃ cup	80 milliliters
¹/₂ cup (4 fluid ounces)	120 milliliters
²/₃ cup	160 milliliters
³/₄ cup	180 milliliters
1 cup (8 fluid ounces)	240 milliliters
1¹/₄ cups	300 milliliters
1¹/₂ cups (12 fluid ounces)	360 milliliters
1²/₃ cups	400 milliliters
2 cups (1 pint)	460 milliliters
3 cups	700 milliliters
4 cups (1 quart)	0.95 liter
1 quart plus ¹/₄ cup	1 liter
4 quarts (1 gallon)	3.8 liters

Weight

¹/₄ ounce	7 grams
¹/₂ ounce	14 grams
³/₄ ounce	21 grams
1 ounce	28 grams
1¹/₄ ounces	35 grams
1¹/₂ ounces	42.5 grams
1²/₃ ounces	45 grams
2 ounces	57 grams
3 ounces	85 grams
4 ounces (¹/₄ pound)	113 grams
5 ounces	142 grams
6 ounces	170 grams
7 ounces	198 grams
8 ounces (¹/₂ pound)	227 grams
16 ounces (1 pound)	454 grams
35.25 ounces (2.2 pounds)	1 kilogram

Length

¹/₈ inch	3 millimeters
¹/₄ inch	6 millimeters
¹/₂ inch	1¹/₄ centimeters
1 inch	2¹/₂ centimeters
2 inches	5 centimeters
2¹/₂ inches	6 centimeters
4 inches	10 centimeters
5 inches	13 centimeters
6 inches	15¹/₄ centimeters
12 inches (1 foot)	30 centimeters

Metric Conversion Formulas

To Convert	Multiply
Ounces to grams	Ounces by 28.35
Pounds to kilograms	Pounds by .454
Teaspoons to milliliters	Teaspoons by 4.93
Tablespoons to milliliters	Tablespoons by 14.79
Fluid ounces to milliliters	Fluid ounces by 29.57
Cups to milliliters	Cups by 236.59
Cups to liters	Cups by .236
Pints to liters	Pints by .473
Quarts to liters	Quarts by .946
Gallons to liters	Gallons by 3.785
Inches to centimeters	Inches by 2.54

Common Ingredients and Their Approximate Equivalents

1 cup uncooked white rice = 185 grams
1 cup all-purpose flour = 140 grams
1 stick butter (4 ounces • 1/2 cup • 8 tablespoons) = 110 grams
1 cup butter (8 ounces • 2 sticks • 16 tablespoons) = 220 grams
1 cup brown sugar, firmly packed = 225 grams
1 cup granulated sugar = 200 grams

Oven Temperatures

To convert Fahrenheit to Celsius, subtract 32 from Fahrenheit, multiply the result by 5, then divide by 9.

Description	Fahrenheit	Celsius	British Gas Mark
Very cool	200°	95°	0
Very cool	225°	110°	1/4
Very cool	250°	120°	1/2
Cool	275°	135°	1
Cool	300°	150°	2
Warm	325°	165°	3
Moderate	350°	175°	4
Moderately hot	375°	190°	5
Fairly hot	400°	200°	6
Hot	425°	220°	7
Very hot	450°	230°	8
Very hot	475°	245°	9

Information compiled from a variety of sources, including *Recipes into Type* by Joan Whitman and Dolores Simon (Newton, MA: Biscuit Books, 2000); *The New Food Lover's Companion* by Sharon Tyler Herbst (Hauppauge, NY: Barron's, 1995); and *Rosemary Brown's Big Kitchen Instruction Book* (Kansas City, MO: Andrews McMeel, 1998).

Index